Charter School
PRIMER

This book is part of the Peter Lang Education list.
Every volume is peer reviewed and meets
the highest quality standards for content and production.

PETER LANG
New York • Washington, D.C./Baltimore • Bern
Frankfurt • Berlin • Brussels • Vienna • Oxford

Anne Marie Tryjankowski

Charter School
PRIMER

PETER LANG
New York • Washington, D.C./Baltimore • Bern
Frankfurt • Berlin • Brussels • Vienna • Oxford

Library of Congress Cataloging-in-Publication Data

Tryjankowski, Anne Marie.
Charter school primer / Anne Marie Tryjankowski.
p. cm. — (Peter Lang primers)
Includes bibliographical references and index.
1. Charter schools—United States. 2. Education and state—United States.
3. School choice—United States. I. Title.
LB2806.36.T79   371.010973—dc23   2011041997
ISBN 978-1-4331-1188-4 (paperback)
ISBN 978-1-4539-0261-5 (e-book)

Bibliographic information published by **Die Deutsche Nationalbibliothek**.
Die Deutsche Nationalbibliothek lists this publication in the "Deutsche
Nationalbibliografie"; detailed bibliographic data is available
on the Internet at http://dnb.d-nb.de/.

The paper in this book meets the guidelines for permanence and durability
of the Committee on Production Guidelines for Book Longevity
of the Council of Library Resources.

© 2012 Peter Lang Publishing, Inc., New York
29 Broadway, 18th floor, New York, NY 10006
www.peterlang.com

Printed in the United States of America

Contents

CHAPTER ONE

What Are Charter Schools?

Overview

In this chapter we will explore the concept of charter schools. Charter schools as a public school choice option are quite controversial. We will examine arguments of proponents of charter schools and arguments of opponents of charter schools. Additionally we will look at common misconceptions about charter schools as educational options and try to clarify those misconceptions.

Charter Schools as Public School Choice Options

Utter the term "charter school" and you will most likely elicit one of three responses—overwhelming support bordering on giddiness that children and families are offered a choice in educational systems, utter disgust that money is being taken away from traditional public schools and that the educational system is being turned into a capitalistic enterprise based on competition, or a blank look of a person totally unfamiliar with the concept.

With the right premise of an argument, the case for the first two of these responses could be made. This primer is an attempt to negate the third response—the "blank look," and present a balanced view of charter schools and their role in American education. We will do this by providing a look at the arguments that surround this educational concept, the history of the movement, legislation governing public charter schools, and the politics of charter schools and groups that have a stake in the movement. We will also look at indicators of success in charter schools, and actually examine one of the many successful models of charter school education in the United States.

What are charter schools? How are students chosen to attend charter schools?

Charter school

Public school authorized by the state to operate independently under the monitoring of a state-approved charter school authorizing agency.

Public lottery

When applications for charter school enrollment exceed the seating capacity of the charter school, the school must hold a public lottery to enroll students.

Public charter school accountability

Charter schools are held accountable for student academic performance, responsible fiscal management, and appropriate governance and stewardship.

Charter schools are public schools, authorized to operate by states and funded by state dollars. They are not private schools. They have no religious affiliation. And as public schools, they cannot discriminate against any student who applies. They cannot accept only the smart students, or the rich students or the white students. Charter schools must open their door, as public schools do, to all students. Of course charter schools have seat limits. They do not have boundless space, and their class size and school size is limited by their agreement with the state in which they operate. Therefore, when applications to a charter school exceed the number of students the charter school can accommodate, a **public lottery** is held to randomly decide which students will be enrolled in the school.

Public charter school accountability is one reason that these schools are often sought out in various reform initiatives. While all public schools are held to academic quality standards, public charter schools are held to an even higher standard of accountability with more severe consequences for not meeting accountability goals. Public charter schools must not only assure that students meet academic goals, but are held to rigorous fiscal and governance standards as well. These accountability standards are set by state legislation and monitored by state charter school authorizers. Public charter schools run the risk of being closed by their authorizer if they fail to meet the standards set for them in any of those three areas.

An additional accountability measure in charter schools is the inherent competitive nature of schools of choice. If parents choose to send their children to a charter school, the school is viable—increasing enrollment and funding. If parents choose to take their children out of a charter school, not only does enrollment decrease, but funding does as well. Charter school funding is based on a per pupil formula, derived uniquely in each state's charter school legislation. So unlike traditional public schools within traditional districts in which money goes to the district as long as the pupil stays within the public school system, schools of choice base their fiscal viability on enrollment.

States have different definitions of the concept of what defines an acceptable student population in charter schools. Some states allow charter schools to state that they will give preference to certain populations of students. These populations often include at-risk populations (defined as students in need of Special Education services or English Language Learners), low-achieving students, students in the district in which the charter school is located, and siblings of students already attending the school. These preferences are delineated in charter school regulations of individual states. The preferences are indicated to allow charter schools to draw from these special populations who are traditionally underserved in public school districts, offering families of these students an alternative manner in which to have their children educated.

How are charter schools created?

Charter schools are created by groups of people who have developed a concept for providing public educational opportunities to students. Groups desiring to open a charter school go through a rigorous application process. The application must include the mission and vision of the school, any special population that the school will focus on serving, the instructional program, how the program will be assessed, how the school will be governed, how students and families will be recruited, how families will be welcomed into the school, how the finances will be monitored. The application is submitted to a state-identified **charter school authorizer.** Successful applicants are granted a **charter.** The charter is typically valid for 3–5 years, and is able to be renewed upon proof of meeting stated academic, fiscal and governance goals.

Charter school authorizer

The entity that is given the power and responsibility to issue charters to charter school founders.

Charter

A charter is an agreement between the state, the state authorizing agency, and the charter school founders to run the public charter school.

Who authorizes charter schools?

Charter school authorizers vary by state and are governed by state charter school legislation. In some states, local boards of education, county boards of education, state boards of education and state boards of regents are authorizers. State education commissioners are authorizers according to some state legislation. Some states have boards of charter schools, or charter school institutes with duties similar to a state school board. Such independent charter schools boards are developed solely for the purpose of authorizing, monitoring and supporting charter schools. Some states allow universities or community colleges to charter schools. Some state charter school legislation gives mayors of large cities within the state to authorize charters within the city they govern. Less common are states where cooperatives, charitable non-profit organizations, educational service provider boards, and education non-profits serve as charter authorizers. Federally recognized Indian tribes are listed as an authorizer for schools within Native American territory in one state.

Requirements for each of these authorizers to become qualified to grant charters to school applicants vary by state. Some states have rigorous standards for their authorizing and oversight organizations, while others have less rigorous standards and are under criticism from proponents and opponents of the charter school movement.

What is a conversion charter school?

Conversion charter school

A traditional public school that is approved to become an independently operated public charter school.

A **conversion charter school** is a school that converts from traditional public to charter public status. Provisions for the creation of a conversion charter school vary by state. This school benefits from decreased mandates and regulations, just as an open-enrollment charter school would. They also gain freedom to create curricular programs and a school culture that meets the needs of their students rather than conforming to district-level policy on these issues. However, just like other charter schools, the trade-off for this freedom is increased accountability. Oftentimes, conversion charters have more restrictions on their operation to assure that students who were previously served by the school continue to be served by the school even when the status changes from traditional to charter public school.

Who starts charter schools and why?

Charter schools are started by individuals, groups, parents, for-profit management companies, not-for-profit organizations, community members, educators, business people, and higher-education institutions. People start charter schools for a variety of reasons. The reasons most often cited for starting a charter school, according to the National Study of Charter Schools (US Department of Education, 2000) was "to seek an alternative vision of schooling that could not be realized in the traditional pub-

Vision of schooling

The mission and goals of a school program.

lic school system." That **vision of schooling** can include such things as unique instructional programs, longer school days and school years, control over utilization of education funding, and the ability to serve at-risk populations in unique ways. The study gives the following statistics: 75.2% of charter schools indicate that one of the reasons they start a charter school is to realize an alternative vision, 30.4% to serve a special population, 16.8% to gain autonomy or flexibility, 9.1% to attract students, 8.9% to increase parent involvement, and 7.5% for financial reasons.

How are charter schools funded?

Public charter schools cannot charge tuition. The schools are **funded publicly**. State dollars support public charter schools in a similar fashion to how they support traditional public schools (these would be city dollars in

Funded publicly

Public funding for charter schools originates from state education funds.

the District of Columbia). Some states pay charter school funds directly to the charter schools. In other cases, money to charters flows through the local school districts from the state. Most states provide charter schools with the per pupil amount of the charter school student's district of residence. In some cases, the amount is less, allowing for administrative costs to be subtracted from that per pupil amount. Funding for public charter school facilities and transportation varies widely by state.

What is a charter school cap?

In some states, there is a **charter school cap** or limit imposed on the number of charter schools that can be

Charter school cap

State limits placed on the number of charter schools that can be authorized.

opened in the state. Sometimes the limits are regionally based, with charter school development being limited to certain regions of the state. Sometimes the limits are on types of charter schools that are allowed to be developed.

For example, certain states allow unlimited development of charter schools that are created to serve students with disabilities.

In his report, *Ideas That Work: Smart Charter School Caps*, Education Sector co-director Andrew Rotherham argues that less attention needs to be paid to the number of charter schools as allowed or denied by charter school caps, and more attention should be paid to growth and quality of schools. He offers the following blueprint for the concept of Smart Charter School Caps. Rather than simply limit the number of charter schools created in a state or by a particular authorizer, Rotherham suggests efforts should be focused on growing successful models of charter schools and charter school authorizers. Charter schools with proven models of success should to be encouraged, replicated and supported. Additionally, state charter school authorizers with the capacity and reputation for high-quality authorizing should also be given the power to authorize without the limit of caps. This focus on issues of quality over issues of quantity will lead to increased high-quality educational choices for families.

Arguments of Proponents and Opponents

Many people are passionate about school reform. The range of caring stakeholders includes parents, teachers, administrators, union executives, local business owners, corporations, non-profit organizations, politicians, Democrats, Republicans, and policy wonks. The list goes on and on. And when it comes to charter school options for education, the stakeholders are quite vocal—and disparate—in their opinions.

Arguments against charter school options

There are many who argue that charter schools are not an appropriate strategy for education reform. Their arguments, as well as counterarguments, of charter school proponents will be explored in this section. The issues include:

+ Public charter schools are able to choose the best and brightest students, leaving struggling or hard-to-educate students in traditional public school districts.

+ Public charter schools are small and do not provide enough seats for all students who want to be enrolled in the school to be able to enroll.
+ Public charter schools are freed from many bureaucratic constraints, mandates and other requirements, giving them an unfair advantage over traditional public schools.
+ Public charter schools take money away from traditional public school systems, decimating programs that could help students in traditional school systems.
+ Some states fund public charter schools at a fraction of the funding of traditional public schools, further widening the educational funding gap between poor, high-need schools and wealthier school districts.
+ When charter schools fail, they are closed. This leaves many students with no continuity of instruction, forcing them to find other schools to attend.
+ Public charter schools do not educate English Language Learners or Students with Disabilities at the same level as traditional public schools, often sending these students back to their traditional public school, thereby avoiding being held accountable for the performance of these **special category high-need students**.

Special category high-need students

Legislatively defined at-risk populations.

+ Public charter schools are an anti-union movement. Union protection is not provided to charter school teachers, resulting in workplaces that are not focused on fair practices for teachers.
+ Strict accountability measures, especially when defined by standardized test scores, leads charter school educators to focus solely on test results in order to remain viable.
+ Introducing a market economy to public education defeats the purpose of a fair, equitable public educational system.
+ Charter schools are money makers for for-profit educational management organizations. Executives are getting rich on taxpayer dollars that are meant to educate children.

Each of these arguments needs to be considered seriously by those who wish to make a valid argument that supports charter school options. As with other issues of charter schools, there are differences in the charter legislation and implementation in each state, so generalizations are offered cautiously.

OPPONENT *concern: Public charter schools are able to choose the best and brightest students, leaving struggling or hard-to-educate students in traditional public school districts.*

While charter schools claim to be open to all applicants, there are certain groups of students who are given preference to attend charter schools. Charter school legislation in some states holds a preference for at-risk students. However additional groups that can be given preference in some charter schools include children of founders of a school, siblings of students already attending the charter school and children of employees of the school. Children of employees of the charter school are also given preference in some states.

While state charter school legislation may seek to maintain open charter school enrollment for all students, allowing families and students equal access to this public education choice, the fact remains that families who apply to charter schools for admittance tend to be families who are concerned enough about their children's education to seek out options to the traditional public school. Such parents tend to be more involved in their children's education and concerned about their children's success. While traditional public school parents are also concerned about providing the best for their children, parents who seek out this public charter school alternative tend to be more aware of options for academic success and more able to follow up on the details of application completion and submission.

This doesn't mean that struggling students or hard-to-educate students are not in charter schools, but it does mean that the level of parent awareness and involvement in these schools tends to ameliorate concerns about struggling students whose parents are not involved in their education.

PROPONENT *counterargument:* The legislation that allows for the creation of public charter schools was intended to allow individuals to create unique educational programs to help at-risk students and students in failing traditional public schools meet learning standards and be better prepared for college and careers.

Charter schools are public schools. As such, they cannot pick their students based on an entrance exam, an interview process, transcript review, or any other selective method. All students who apply must be admitted. When schools are enrolled to capacity, a public lottery must be held to randomly select students to fill the seats in the school. There are some conditions that may give students applying to a charter school preference in their application. Lotteries can give preference to one set of students over another through a weighting process. This is permitted when a school needs to comply with Title VI of the Civil Rights Act of 1964, Title IX of the Education Amendments of 1972, Section 504 of the Rehabilitation Act of 1973, the Equal Protection Clause of the Constitution, or applicable State law (from Charter Schools Program Title V, Part B, Non-Regulatory Guidance). Some states require that preference be given to low-achieving students. In some states, preference is given to students who reside in the city/town in which the school exists. Dependent children of active military personnel are sometimes given preferred enrollment status.

Charter schools are typically located in areas where traditional public schools are struggling. They are presented as an alternative for families who are not satisfied with the education their children are receiving in the traditional public school system. In communities where public schools are thriving—typically upper-middle-class and upper-class communities—there is less public demand for educational alternatives. In these communities, the school system is meeting the needs of all learners, providing extracurricular options, and per pupil funding is appropriate to adequately educate students. Additionally, upper-middle-class and upper-class families also have the means to send their children to private schools, and pay tuition in those schools, if they are not satisfied with their district schools.

Instead, charter schools are typically created in communities where instructional supplies are often lacking, where funding is not appropriately allocated to meet the needs of students and teachers, and where student failure is the norm. It is these families that charter schools are looking to enroll in their academic programs. Most charter schools are created to meet the needs of these traditionally underserved populations.

Charter school advocates do find that there is some attempt at elitism in some schools. Some charters are created to give upper-middle-class and upper-class families a public school option within failing traditional public school systems. These attempts are looked down upon by most charter school operators who exist to serve more traditional high-need charter populations, and legislation dictating open-enrollment and high-need preferences in charter school applications exist in an attempt to minimize such elitist attempts.

OPPONENT concern: Public charter schools are small and do not provide enough seats for all students who want to be enrolled in the school to be able to enroll. Public charter schools can be large or small. However, popular movies like *The Lottery* or *Waiting for Superman* magnify the fact that not all families and students who would like to be enrolled in certain public charter schools can be enrolled due to limited enrollment capacity of those schools. In these movies, families who are frustrated with the traditional public schools their child(ren) must attend, seek to enroll their children in charter schools with a reputation for success. Because the application pool for the high-quality charter schools exceeds the number of seats, the students' names are entered in a lottery. The audience in each of these movies learns about each family and their motivation for desiring public charter school choice for their children. The children are also interviewed and share what enrollment in the school will mean to them. Movie audiences then watch the lottery unfold—seeing the faces of relief and jubilation on those who get chosen for a place in the charter school—and the look of disappointment and despair in those who don't.

The level of disappointment repeats itself annually throughout the states with charter legislation, as the seating capacity of successful charter schools is overwhelmed by the number of families submitting applications for enrollment in the school. This is a case of limited supply and high demand. Successful schools draw more applications than they can possibly accept, and lotteries often leave families disappointed.

PROPONENT counterargument: Efforts have been made to try to replicate successful charter school models through a variety of avenues, including provision of funding for **"replication schools"**—schools that re-create successful programs in other charter schools to increase "supply" of seats for students and families who desire certain public charter school choice options.

Replication schools

School models that have proven successful and are encouraged to create additional schools under the same model.

The argument that there is not enough space for all students and families who desire a charter school education is an argument FOR charter schools—for their importance in the community and their efficacy at providing opportunities for students to succeed. Charter school waiting lists are often used to illustrate that public charter school choice is an option that families desire.

This is also an argument about the importance of raising charter school caps in states. Parents, as taxpayers in a state, have the right to send their children to the schools that they feel will provide the best educational opportunities for academic success. When states limit the number or type of public charter schools within the state, parents have limited choices when opting for a public school. Raising charter school caps would provide charter school operators with the freedom to open schools, and would increase enrollment opportunities in public charter schools, negating the argument that only a limited number of families are served by the public charter school option.

OPPONENT concern: Public charter schools are freed from many bureaucratic constraints, mandates and other requirements, giving them an unfair advantage over traditional public schools. Charter schools are given freedom from some bureaucratic mandates in exchange for increased accountability. Having this freedom allows a charter school to focus on innovation and student success. If traditional public schools were given equal freedoms from mandates and other requirements, they would also be able to spend more of their human resources on instructional innovation, providing opportunities for student success and making them more competitive with charter schools.

PROPONENT counterargument: In exchange for freedom from bureaucratic constraints and mandates, public charter schools are held to a high standard of accountability. The accountability is not only academic in nature. Traditional public schools and public charter schools are all held to high academic standards per the No Child Left Behind (NCLB) Act. NCLB has sanctions for low-performing schools, be they traditional public schools or public charter schools.

In addition to NCLB accountability, public charter schools are held to high standards in the areas of **academic accountability, fiscal accountability** and **governance accountability.** Charter plans must include accountability

Academic accountability

The manner in which a school is held responsible for student learning.

Fiscal accountability

The manner in which a school is held responsible for appropriate expenditures of public funds.

Governance accountability

The manner in which a board is held responsible for making policy decisions and school leadership decisions.

measures for each of these areas that go beyond the NCLB requirements. Charter authorizers monitor public charter schools to assure compliance with these established standards. If a public charter school fails to meet the accountability standard set at any one of these levels, the school is in danger of being closed.

As a school of choice, a charter school also has the added accountability of drawing a student population in order to procure funding for program. Without meeting its enrollment goals, a public charter school risks not having enough funds to meet its fiscal responsibility within the specified program development.

OPPONENT concern: Public charter schools take money away from traditional public school systems, decimating programs that could help students in traditional school systems. In some states, local school districts have to take money from their operating budget and transfer it to charter schools where district students are enrolled. In other states, the funding comes directly from the state; however, a district that loses students to charter schools has a lower student enrollment population and therefore gets less funding than it would if all students in the municipality were enrolled in a traditional district public school. Losing enrollment to a charter school does not necessarily reduce costs proportionally. School buildings must still be maintained, lit, heated and air-conditioned. Central office responsibilities do not decrease, because curriculum, professional development, human resources, purchasing and other services remain as constant costs. Expenditures remain steady despite the loss of students. There are no economies of scale realized through student migration to public charter schools. And funding lost to these charter schools is funding taken away from programs for students in the traditional public school system.

PROPONENT counterargument: Public dollars for education should be used to educate children. If a family chooses to enroll in a public charter school, the money designated for the education of that student should go to the public charter school. Parents who choose to send their children to public charter schools are voting with their tax dollars and choosing the option that best serves their children.

In some states, the home district of the charter school student retains a percentage of the per pupil expenditure received for charter school students. The entire per pupil expenditure does not follow the child. This method of school funding enables the district to cover fixed costs at the district level, even though they are not educating the child who is in the charter school. This method of funding is seen as unfair to, and by, charter school supporters, because charter schools also have administrative expenses that need to be addressed. Many public charter schools are required to offer innovative programs with increased accountability at lower levels of per pupil funding.

OPPONENT concern: Some states fund public charter schools at a fraction of the funding of traditional public schools, further widening the educational funding gap between poor, high-need schools and wealthier school districts. While some states fund public charter school students at the full per pupil expenditure of traditional public school students, some do not. Those states that do not provide equal funding—including lack of funding for transportation, facilities or other school basics—do, in fact, widen a gap. Most public charter schools are created in districts where schools and students are already struggling. These schools tend to exist in high-need urban areas. Total school funding in these districts tends to be lower than in wealthier suburban districts. A lower funding formula for charter schools creates a fiscal situation where some of the most disadvantaged students in charter schools are getting fewer dedicated educational dollars than disadvantaged students in underperforming traditional public schools. The fear is that charter school funding formulas may create an even less-equitable educational system than already exists.

PROPONENT counterargument: The funding inequity is a concern to charter school operators and proponents. Even in states where the per pupil expenditure follows the student with no administrative costs taken out for the district, there are other inequities that exist. Transportation aid and building aide are often left out of charter school funding formulas, leaving charter schools to figure out a way to finance those costs from their already-meager funds. And yet many charter schools are successful despite the inequity of funding. A charter school proponent may argue that throwing more money at the problem of poor education will not solve the problem. Rather, a different system for delivery of educational services, even with less funding, may be a reasonable alternative.

OPPONENT concern: When charter schools fail, they are closed. This leaves many students with no continuity of instruction, forcing them to find other schools to attend. Charter school opponents point to the argument that continuity of instruction program and the stability of attending a school that does not face the threat of closure is important in any child's life, and even more important for a child who lives in poverty. Since charter schools typically receive a charter for the length of 3 to 5 years, renewable, there is always the threat that the school will close if it does not meet the accountability goals as defined in the charter. When a school closes, an entire population of students and families must rush to make accommodations for the following year. At this point, enrollment in another charter school may be difficult, especially given the public lottery process. And enrollment in the traditional public school is an option that was not palatable to these families when they first enrolled in the charter school. These families may now be left with no viable options for their children's education.

PROPONENT counterargument: Public charter schools are created as a public school choice option for families whose children attend failing traditional public schools. This option was created to support the belief that families should not have to attend schools that do not provide adequate educational opportunities for their children. Even the staunchest proponent of public charter school choice would argue that children should not be enrolled in failing schools, even if those schools are failing charter schools. The impetus behind the movement is the creation of schools that deliver successful educational experiences for children. If such schools fail to deliver, they should be closed.

Proponents would also argue that current federal legislation also calls for the closing of traditional public schools that are failing. These schools are given opportunities to reconfigure their program in an attempt to improve. If necessary improvements are not realized, the school has various options including conversion to a charter school, replacement of the educational leader, replacement of half of the teaching staff of the school or closure. The threat of school closure is real in traditional public school districts as well. However, the stakes are a bit lower for the adults in the system in these cases. The closure of a traditional public school still ensures teacher protection under their collective bargaining agreement. Teachers with seniority in the system will retain positions within the system, regardless of their ability to deliver instruction in meaningful ways. But students are still forced into changing schools and interrupting the continuity of instruction, just as would happen if a public charter school failed to perform.

OPPONENT concern: Public charter schools do not educate English Language Learners or Students with Disabilities at the same level as traditional public schools, often sending these students back to their traditional public school, thereby avoiding being held accountable for the performance of these special category high-need students. Charter schools are often accused of not appropriately providing services for English Language Learners or Student with Disabilities. Opponents of public charter school choice point out that these students, when enrolled in charter schools, are often not appropriately educated, and in some instances actually advised to return to their district of residence for instruction. Accountability measures typically require that these high-service students still be measured in a school's annual yearly progress goals. By not including these students in the instructional program and assessment protocol, public charter schools have an unfair advantage in reporting student growth over the traditional district that is required to educate and assess these students.

PROPONENT counterargument: Most proponents of public charter school choice are concerned about meeting special needs of students. Legislation in many states gives special consideration to enrollment of at-risk students including students living in poverty, students with special needs, and English Language Learners. Legislation in some states also requires proof of recruitment initiatives that target at-risk students.

One of the challenges that public charter schools face in meeting the prescribed needs of Students with Disabilities and English Language Learners is that there is an inherent challenge to serve these students without centralized support. The nature of charter schools is that they are independent of a central office bureaucracy, and unless part of a network of schools, do not have other schools with which to legally partner in the area of special service provision. Without the organizational capacity to service these learners, resources are not necessarily available to satisfy federal- and state-level requirements for student services.

Let's take, for example, a small charter school with an enrollment of a few students with disabilities. In this school, as often happens, there are not enough students in need of the same level of service enrolled. When this happens in traditional public school districts, students requiring similar levels of service are moved to one school where the service is available. This is not possible when a student is enrolled in a public charter school. Consider the following specifics. A public charter school has one child enrolled in first grade in the school requiring a classroom with four students, one teacher and one teacher assistant. Another child enrolled in the school at the seventh grade level requires an educational setting with fifteen students and one teacher. And another child in seventh grade requires a setting with four students, one teacher and one teacher aide. Needing to keep the students in the least restrictive environment, the school could not create an appropriate learning program for these students. That leaves two options—a parent can enroll the child in a school where an appropriate learning program can be put in place. Or the parent can waive required special services and keep the child in the charter school. Neither of these options is ideal. However, unless a public charter school has the capability to provide appropriate services to these students, there is no other option.

A report from Project Intersect from the University of Maryland was commissioned to study special education in charter schools. They find that the independent nature of charter schools leaves them to struggle with finding the capacity to comply with federal Individuals with Disabilities Act (IDEA) requirements at the organizational, legal and fiscal levels.

The Project Intersect researchers studied various structures that charter schools are employing to help themselves build capacity as they provide services to students with disabilities. The researchers studied structures where the authorizer provided infrastructure, where charter schools shared a director of special education services and training, where charter schools formed a special education cooperative, and where private special education service companies provided the infrastructure. They found strengths and challenges associated with each model, and through their case study analysis, they found several recurrent themes. Specifically, charter schools must understand their state's policy context, must identify the needs they have regarding special education infrastructure, identify external resources, utilize effective leadership, and establish explicit roles and responsibilities and leverage mutual interests with other educational service providers (charter and non-charter schools).

OPPONENT concern: Public charter schools are an anti-union movement. Union protection is not provided to charter school teachers, resulting in workplaces that are not focused on fair practices for teachers. Protection of public charter school teachers by the local teacher union contract is not always guaranteed. Some states require that the charter school be bound by the local school district teacher contract. Other states do not guarantee such contract protection. And yet other state legislation binds a charter school to the local contract, with the ability to make changes to the contract per the charter or per charter school employee vote. The lack of a common belief in the importance of unions in public charter schools is of concern. Charter school teachers are not given the benefits of collective bargaining. Most charter school teachers are considered **"at will" employees**, meaning that their employment can be terminated at any time with no reason given. In addition to the benefits of collective bargaining, unions are beneficial in that they create a formal process by which concerns about management can be brought forward and dealt with. This formal process does not exist in the charter school movement, further challenging the teachers' ability to make changes in the school that would better serve children.

PROPONENT counterargument: Charter schools are held to high standards of accountability. If charter schools do not increase academic success of their enrolled students, they may be closed by their authorizer. As such, it is essential that charter schools retain only high quality educators. If a teacher does not engage students in an instructional plan that results in student learning, the school program is in jeopardy. At-will employment allows charter school leaders and governing boards to employ the best teachers and leaders available to ensure student success.

At-will employees

At-will employees can be terminated from their position anytime for any reason, except for reasons that are prohibited by state and federal law.

But at-will employment is not the situation everywhere in the charter world and only one issue in the union debate over charter schools. Many charter schools are operating under union contracts. Those union contracts are not necessarily the contracts of the district teacher union in which the school is located. Rather many schools vote to amend the union contract or create their own unions and negotiate their own contracts. It is not union involvement or collective bargaining that should be the central question for charter schools.

OPPONENT concern: Strict accountability measures, especially when defined by standardized test scores, lead charter school educators to focus solely on test results in order to remain viable. If failure to attain accountability standards results in the closing of a charter school, one can make the assumption that the charter school will go to any length to assure that those accountability standards are met. Opponents voicing this concern fear that accountability standards, typically equating success in education to success on standardized tests, force charter schools to narrowly focus on standardized testing as opposed to a whole-child education. And while federal and state definitions of student success typically equate to success on standardized tests for all public schools, the threat of closure and job loss in a charter school provides a unique opportunity for a narrow educational focus.

PROPONENT counterargument: Federal No Child Left Behind legislation imposes strict sanctions for schools that do not raise achievement levels of students. After providing opportunities to restructure to better meet the needs of students, the schools can be subject to closing. This is no different than the accountability in public charter schools. One can only hope that public charter schools and traditional public schools will take their professional responsibility seriously enough to provide outstanding learning opportunities for children that will, in fact, also help children succeed when assessed via standardized testing methods.

OPPONENT concern: Introducing a market economy to public education defeats the purpose of a fair, equitable public educational system. There are opponents to charter schools who focus on the ideology that competition in public education undermines the power of working-class solidarity. In doing so, there is no public universal education in this capitalist model.

PROPONENT counterargument: It is important to have strong public schools for all students. The ideal situation would be to have traditional public school systems that met the needs of students in a unique and engaging manner. However, the systems appear to be broken in some areas. And it is in those geographic areas that charter schools tend to be created. While adults work tirelessly to try to fix the broken school systems, parents have to remember that children get only one chance to be in any grade. And they need to find schools that will give their children the best chance to get ahead. Charter proponents would also argue that perhaps the charter movement is only a temporary movement, one that creates enough momentum and competition so that the traditional public school districts become better and create schools that compete for students who are enrolled in charter schools, creating stronger traditional public school systems.

OPPONENT concern: Charter schools are money-makers for for-profit educational management organizations. Executives are getting rich on tax-payer dollars that are meant to educate children. The idea of competition turns the pure institution of free public education to a private enterprise, tempting many for-profits to provide services at the expense of tax-payers, and make money at the expense of our children's education.

PROPONENT counterargument: Public charter schools do not have the support of a central district office to manage issues like curriculum, assessment, human resources and financing. In order to appropriately comply with various mandates and administrative tasks, some charter schools find that purchasing these services from a high-quality service provider with experience in the field is the most efficient way to handle these administrative tasks. Some public charter schools handle these tasks on their own, or with the assistance of non-profit educational firms. But those who choose **for-profit management companies** benefit from the high quality of services provided due to the free-market service provision inherent in most charter schools.

For-profit education management companies

Businesses that provide educational services in order to make a profit for the company owners and investors.

Moving forward

This presentation of a few of the arguments for and against charter schools leads one to believe that some misinformation exists in the public sector about this school choice option. And even when information is correct, people have strong feelings about this issue based on ideology and practicality.

The remainder of the charter school primer will explore the history of charter schools, the legislation and politics that affect charter schools, what charter schools look like today, and what course they are traveling in the future of education reform.

Chapter Summary

Charter schools are public schools receiving funding from the state. Each state that authorizes charter schools has unique legislation that sets the stage for charter school development within the state. State regulations can give preference to charter schools that target high-need or at-risk populations.

There are strong proponents and strong critics of the charter school movement. Proponents point to strong accountability measures, innovative instruction, independent governance, and parent support as key factors in the need for sustaining the momentum of the charter school movement. Opponents are concerned about charter schools as an anti-union movement, a movement that threatens public education, and a drain on traditional school district dollars.

GLOSSARY

Charter school—A public school that is authorized by the state to operate independently of the traditional public school district, but under the monitoring of a state-approved charter school authorizing agency.

Public charter school lottery—When applications for charter school enrollment exceed the seating capacity of the charter school, the school must hold a public lottery to enroll students. State legislation dictates any weighting in a lottery, like sibling preference, residing in city where the school exists, or specifically defined high-need preference.

Public charter school accountability—Charter schools are held accountable for student academic performance, responsible fiscal management, and appropriate governance and stewardship. The concept of accountability is emphasized when discussing charter schools because the sanction for non-compliance with accountability standards is typically revocation of the charter resulting in the school being closed.

Charter—A charter is an agreement between the state, the state authorizing agency, and the charter school founders to run the public charter school. The charter states the regulations and accountability measures to which the charter school will be held accountable.

Charter school authorizer—The entity that is given the power and responsibility to issue charters to charter school founders. The authorizers are held to accountability standards per individual state charter school legislation.

Conversion charter school—A traditional public school that is approved to become an independently operated public charter school. A conversion charter school is no longer under the governance of the traditional public school board, but is independently governed by its own board. State charter school legislation dictates any unique regulations that apply to conversion charter schools.

Vision of schooling—The mission and goals of a school program.

Funded publicly—Public funding for charter schools originates from state education funds. Charter schools are also eligible for certain federal education funds.

Special category high-need students—These at-risk populations are defined as such in the individual state charter school laws.

Replication schools—School models that have proven successful and are encouraged to create additional schools under the same model.

Charter school cap—State limits placed on the number of charter schools that can be authorized. Not all states have charter school caps.

Academic accountability—The manner in which a school is held responsible for student learning. This is typically measured by student performance on standardized tests, as well as other identified measures.

Fiscal accountability—The manner in which a school is held responsible for appropriate expenditures of public funds

Governance accountability—The manner in which a board is held responsible for making policy decisions and school leadership decisions.

At-will employees—At-will employees can be terminated from their position anytime for any reason, except for reasons that are prohibited by state and federal law.

For-profit education management companies—Businesses that provide educational services, including running schools, in order to make a profit for the company owners and investors.

CHAPTER TWO

History of Charter Schools

Overview of the Chapter

In this chapter we will examine various movements and philosophies that led to the concept of charter schools. Then we will at the look at the birth of the movement including the first states that enacted charter school legislation, as well as federal support of charter schools. We'll look at how the movement grew throughout the United States.

Charter schools—not an entirely new concept

The concept of the public charter school choice is really a culmination of a variety of other school reforms that have been implemented over the years. In the 1960s, **magnet schools** were a reform movement created to increase racial desegregation in the United States. **Magnet schools** are public choice options within traditional public school districts. Magnet schools develop unique curricular programs to draw students and families to want to enroll. They have school enrollment policies that target a diverse student body. Staff is trained in unique methodologies to be able to deliver instruction in support of the unique curriculum.

Magnet schools

Theme-based public schools of choice.

Small Schools Project

An initiative to create smaller learning communities in public schools through theme-based learning and strong adult-student relationships.

School-based decision-making

A process by which teams of stakeholders make school decisions at the school level.

Site-based management

A process by which teams of stakeholders make school decisions at the school level.

Decentralized decision-making

The distribution of decision-making power throughout a group or organization, instead of focused at the top of the organization.

Albert Shanker (1928–1997)

A civil rights activist, union leader, and vocal proponent of education reform, and president of the American Federation of Teachers (AFT) in 1974.

The **Small Schools Project** is a reform movement that promotes the development of small communities of learning that focus on student learning through relevant learning experiences for students and strong teacher-student connections. The schools are small in enrollment. They are created around a central theme, very much like a magnet school. Great emphasis is place on adult-student interactions, with daily student advisories, and maintaining advisor relationship throughout an entire high school career being common. Some small schools are created as small populations of schools in single facilities. Other small schools are created as interest-based academies within a larger school community. But all have the commonality of theme-based interactive learning and the development of strong relationships with significant adults. These schools, like magnet schools and public charter schools, are schools of choice. Students and families choose to attend the school based on the quality and reputation of the learning program.

School-based decision-making, **site-based management** and **decentralized decision-making** are other reform models that have been implemented as a tool to lessen the centralization of power in traditional public education systems. In these models of decision-making, decision making authority comes from the school, or the local site at which educational services are delivered. In pure school-based, or site-based decision-making models, school teams make decisions about programming in their school, school culture, leadership, professional development and budgeting and are held accountable for student results.

These precursors to charter schools had in place a variety of features that informed the charter school model.

As we begin to talk about the actual inception of the public charter school movement, one would assume a discussion of **Albert Shanker** and his suggestions to have a union-approved, independently run school would lead the text. However, it is an interesting point to note that the term "charter school" was used as far back as 1733, in an attempt to convert Irish Catholics to Protestants. We find in Hassencamp's *History of Ireland from the Reformation to the Union* (1888), that not only were Catholics banned from the university, but they were also prevented from opening a school or teaching in one.

The Irish Catholics were therefore compelled either to allow their children to grow up in utter ignorance, or to send them to the Charter Schools, institutions founded by Primate Boulter in 1733, mainly for the purpose of making proselytes.

This dignitary of the English Church regarded it as his especial mission "to bring over by all Christian means, the great mass of Irish Papists into the Church of England, and he conceived that the most effectual means of doing this would be the establishment of the Charter Schools, which, according to the published programme, were founded to rescue the souls of thousands of poor children from the dangers of popish superstition and idolatry, and their bodies from the miseries of idleness and beggary. Nor is it to be denied that those institutions were remarkably well calculated to ensure conversions. The children of poor parents were here gratuitously boarded, lodged, clothed, and educated; the boys were apprenticed to some trade and the girls placed in situations, and even a small dowry apportioned to the latter; but this was all associated with the sole and inviolable condition that the children should be educated in the Protestant faith. And so much exasperation did this single stipulation create that Irish parents seldom willingly sent their children to these schools. In times of famine these richly endowed establishments were better attended, but immediately the distress was over, the schools were again deserted; and as a proof of the aversion with which the population of Ireland regarded this violence done to their consciences, it has been stated that even during the present century, the Irish peasant seldom passed the school without a curse, or a heart-felt sigh of anguish."

And while a cynic could make unfavorable comparisons between the Protestant charter schools of 1733 and the public charter schools of today, let us hope that this scenario is not what Albert Shanker had in mind when he supported the initial idea of charter schools. There is some bit of myth around the irony of a union leader being one of the first advocates to conceive of the notion of public charter school choice in education. Perhaps the story closer to the truth is that as a young teacher, Shanker became concerned about his experience with the lack of respect for the exuberance of young teachers by school administrators. He is reported to have felt that teachers needed more of a say in school instructional program. He supported the idea of creating a school that was approved by the union and teachers to run independently of any central office administration. However, he did not advocate for the school to be outside of the district, nor did he imagine that contracts negotiated by teachers would come to be seen as obstacles to delivering public education.

Supporting Shanker's desire for charter schools adding value to the educational process through respect for teacher innovation, another union leader, Randi Weingarten, is noted as saying, "To get better schools we have to learn how to merge teachers' commitments to their daily work with the spirit of entrepreneurship. Today there is too little entrepreneurship within the school district structure and too little [teacher] professionalism in charter schools" (Hill, Rainey and Rotherham, 2006; *The Future of Charter Schools and Teachers Unions—Results of a Symposium.* p. 2).

Shanker actually supported this idea as developed by Ray Budde (1988) in his paper "Education by Charter, Restructuring School Districts." Budde makes the case for school reform by presenting a framework of goals that a district would embrace in order to reorganize for change in school district structure. First, teachers would take control of instruction. Additional goals included ensuring that students take responsibility for their behavior and learning; linking professional growth to the needs of the school/district; extending the school year from 10 to 12 months; providing teachers with the opportunity to take on professional-level, non-classroom responsibilities as part of their careers; ensuring budgeting to allow educational programs to be planned and implemented in a 3–5-year time frame; enabling principals to take on the role of supporting teachers in instruction and creating safe learning environments; establishing a program evaluation system that is independent and external to the programs being evaluated; promoting understanding of research-based changes in knowledge and instruction; utilizing computer technology and advance communication strategies; integrating educational research into the school culture; and encouraging the participation of all stakeholders (parents and community members) in the education of children. (Budde 1988).

The charter education model proposed by Budde was further developed with a blueprint for implementation. The main tenets of current public charter school legislation are evident in his goals for reorganization—local control;

student responsibility; budgets for program implementation; principals as instructional leaders; research based; technology integration; and active community participation. It would be hard to argue that these goals are anything but positive for transforming educational systems. So where did the conflict come into play?

Initial public charter school legislation at the state levels

Initial charter school legislation in Minnesota, as described below, met most of the tenet's of Budde's work, supported by Shanker. In November of 1988 the **Citizens League of Minneapolis, Minnesota** issued a report called *Chartered Schools = Choices for Educators + Quality for All Students.* (The Citizens League is: The Citizens League builds civic imagination and capacity in Minnesota by:

Citizens League of Minneapolis, Minnesota

A group created to build "civic infrastructure" by framing policy problems, developing civic leaders and building relationships to achieve their goals.

- Identifying, framing and proposing solutions to public policy problems;
- Developing civic leaders in all generations who govern for the common good; and
- Organizing the individual and institutional relationships necessary to achieve these goals.)

The group prided their state on not simply trying to inflict tougher standards on traditional school districts, but rather on providing incentives and opportunities to give schools a reason and a way to become better. To build on that pride, the Citizens League recommended that the state authorize an alternative structure for school governance. The committee presented the concept of chartered public schools. They recommend that:

A chartered school is one granted a "charter" by either a school district of the state to be different in the way it delivers education, and within broad guidelines, to be autonomous. It need not be a school building. It may result in several schools in one building. It is the process of schooling and not the building itself that will differentiate a chartered school from a conventional one.

The chartered school concept recognizes that different children learn in different ways and at different speeds, and teachers and schools should adapt to children's needs rather than requiring children to adapt to the standard system.

A chartered school is a public school and would serve all children. Students would be integrated by ability level and race. Chartered schools could not select only the best and the brightest students or the easiest to teach.

Although chartered schools would have a freedom to pursue different educational routes, they would be operated by licensed educators, would meet accreditation standards and would meet desegregation rules.

In 1991, the Minnesota Legislature passed the first version of charter school legislation *Laws of Minnesota 1991*, chapter 265, article 9, section 3. This legislation established Outcome-Based Schools. The purpose of these schools was very similar to the organizational goals of Budde. "The purpose of the section is to: (1) improve pupil learning; (2) increase learning opportunities for pupils; (3) encourage the use of different and innovative teaching methods; (4) require the measurement of learning outcomes and create different and innovative forms of measuring outcomes; (5) establish new forms of accountability for schools; or (6) create new professional opportunities for teachers, including the opportunity to be responsible for the learning program at the school site."

This law was the first legislation in the United States to allow for the creation of public charter schools. The law specifically gives teachers the authority to open schools—called **Outcome-Based Schools** in the initial legislation. The legislation is very prescriptive in stating who can open these schools, the demographics of advisory board members, the right to organize under collective bargaining, and the accountability for student performance. Two schools received charters in Minnesota in 1992—Bluffview Montessori School in Winona, MN and City Academy in St. Paul, MN.

Outcome-based schools

Schools created by teachers with the assistance of advisory boards. Outcome-based schools in Minnesota were the first public charter schools in the United States.

Other states followed this path of public school choice. The table below indicates the 40 states and District of Columbia that have charter school legislation and the year in which the legislation was passed.

Let's revisit the question posed earlier in this chapter. Budde proposed and Shanker supported the idea of a chartered school, a school where teacher innovation was rewarded with local control and challenged to increased accountability. As the charter movement began to grow, opening a charter school was no longer limited to teachers—as was clearly stated in the first legislation in Minnesota. More freedom was provided in legislation as to the makeup of founding groups. Some educators who

Year Charter Law Passes	State	Year Charter Law Passes	State
1991	Minnesota	1996	Connecticut
1992	California		Florida
1993	Colorado		New Jersey
	Georgia		North Carolina
	Massachusetts		South Carolina
	Michigan	1997	Mississippi
	New Mexico		Nevada
	Wisconsin		Ohio
1994	Arizona		Pennsylvania
	Hawaii	1998	Idaho
	Kansas		Missouri
1995	Alaska		New York
	Arkansas		Utah
	Delaware		Virginia
	District of Columbia	1999	Oklahoma
	Louisiana		Oregon
	New Hampshire	2001	Indiana
	Rhode Island	2002	Iowa
	Texas		Tennessee
	Wyoming	2003	Maryland
		2009	Illinois

were opening schools found that they had solid ideas for instructional programs, but lacked other administrative expertise. Some non-educators found that they could open schools that were structurally sound from a business and finance perspective, but they had no curricular expertise. With this need made increasingly evident, **Educational Management Organizations** (EMOs) began to be formed with the purpose of contracting services to these innovators who have opened charter schools without well-balanced levels of expertise.

Charter legislation then began to support the concept of an EMO actually opening a public charter school. EMOs, or **Educational Service Providers** (ESPs) are looked upon favorably by some proponents of charter schools. The model charter school law, as developed by the National Alliance for Public Charter Schools (A New Model Law for Supporting the Growth of High-Quality Public Charter Schools, 2009) includes the inclusion of ESPs among its essential components. They provide the condition that there should be a "clear performance contract between the

Educational Management Organizations

Organizations that assist in the creation and management of public charter schools.

Educational Service Providers

Organizations that provide contracted services to public charter schools.

independent public charter school board and the service provider and there are no conflicts of interest between the two entities." They cite the rationale for inclusion of this component as the history of the role that these organizations (ESPs) have played in opening and operating charter schools.

In their database ranking current state charter legislation, high marks are given to those states whose legislation includes the following components in regards to ESPs.

10a. All types of educational service providers (both for-profit and non-profit) explicitly allowed to operate all or parts of schools.

10b. The charter application requires 1) performance data for all current and past schools operated by the ESP, including documentation of academic achievement and (if applicable) school management success; and 2) explanation and evidence of the ESP's capacity for successful growth while maintaining quality in existing schools.

10c. A performance contract is required between the independent public charter school board and the ESP, setting forth material terms including but not limited to: performance evaluation measures; methods of contract oversight and enforcement by the charter school board; compensation structure and all fees to be paid to the ESP; and conditions for contract renewal and termination.

10d. The material terms of the ESP performance contract must be approved by the authorizer prior to charter approval.

10e. School governing boards operating as entities completely independent of any educational service provider (e.g., must retain independent oversight authority of their charter schools, and cannot give away their authority via contract).

10f. Existing and potential conflicts of interest between the two entities are required to be disclosed and explained in the charter application. (http://charterlaws.publiccharters.org/charterlaws/component/10, retrieved 6/2/2011)

State legislation on this issue varies. Some states are silent on the ESP provision of service model, with nothing preventing ESPs from providing services. Other states explicitly allow ESP services, but do not require contracts or evidence of capacity in the legislation.

We can conclude that while market need led to the rise of this method of contracting services for managing charter schools, it was not the original intent of an expectation of Budde's original proposal for chartered education, Shanker's support of the concept, or Minnesota's initial legislation on the creation of outcome-based schools.

Federal support of charter schools

Authorization of Title X of the Elementary and Secondary Education Act (ESEA) in 1994

Elementary and Secondary Act (ESEA)

A U.S. federal law initially passed in 1965 and reauthorized every five years. The original purpose of ESEA was to improve educational opportunities for poor children.

While charter school legislation is a state-level enactment, there has been federal support of the charter school movement. Congress authorized Title X of the **Elementary and Secondary Education Act (ESEA)** in 1994, which created the Public Charter Schools Program. This program funded the planning, implementation and start-up of new charter schools.

This legislation was amended by H.R. 2616 and in 1998, President Clinton signed the **Charter School Expansion Act of 1998** into law. His goal was for the creation of 3,000 chartered schools by the year 2002. Under this new law, funding to states was predicated upon several conditions. There was priority given to states that: required charters to be evaluated every five years to ensure that the goals of the charter were being met; increased the number of high-quality charter schools; required the use of the same standardized assessments in public charter schools that were required in traditional public schools; recognized successful charter schools as models of other public charter and traditional public schools.

Charter School Expansion Act of 1998

An amendment of Titles VI and X of ESEA 1965 to improve and expand charter schools.

No Child Left Behind (NCLB)

No Child Left Behind (NCLB) Act

A reauthorization of the 1965 ESEA focused on holding states accountable for academic progress of all students as measured by a school's adequate yearly progress. Schools failing to make such progress were sanctioned under this act.

The passage of the **No Child Left Behind Act** in 2002 redefined consequences for schools that were not performing according to preset criteria. With the passage of NCLB, schools and districts had increased accountability for academic performance outcomes. Along with required annual assessments, schools that did not make specific benchmarks of adequate yearly progress (AYP) were subject to specific consequences for lack of academic performance. Lack of performance would result in specified restructuring of the failing school. Restructuring efforts must be consistent with the state laws, but NCLB specifies that options include: reopening as a public charter school; replacing "all or most of the staff (which may include the principal) who are relevant to the failure to make adequate yearly progress"; contracting with "an outside entity, such as a private management company with a demonstrated record of effectiveness, to operate a school"; turning the "operation of the school over to the state educational agency, if permitted under State law and agreed to by the State"; engaging in another form of major restructuring that makes fundamental reform, "such as significant changes in the school's staffing and governance, to improve student academic achievement in the school and that has substantial promise of enabling the school to make adequate yearly progress." (No Child Left Behind Act, 2002)

The NCLB Act had many implications for the public charter school movement. First, parents of children in low-performing schools were given an option to remove their children from the low-performing school, with a choice being charter school enrollment; second, charter schools had an additional layer of accountability with which to contend; and third, districts were give the option to turn low-performing schools into charter schools. We will deal with each of these issues separately.

Parents of children in low-performing schools. NCLB gives parents in failing schools a way to remove their child from a failing school. According to the NCLB Act, a school that does not make adequate yearly progress for two consecutive school years is identified as a school in need of improvement. The Act requires the school to enter into a planning phase and implement a two-year plan to improve the academic performance of the school. The school must also offer students in the school the opportunity to transfer to a school that is not low performing. The option could be another district school or a public charter school. This school choice option must be offered to parents in low-performing schools until the school turns around and becomes a school that is making AYP. Under NCLB, this school choice option is also in place for any child attending a "persistently dangerous school" as defined by state law, or any child who has been the victim of a violent crime which has occurred on school grounds.

Additional layer of charter school accountability. While a charter school advocate may argue that the ultimate level of accountability for a charter school—closing for lack of academic performance, financial management or governance—is strong enough accountability for the movement, the very specific prescriptions of NCLB add precise benchmarks for achievement and remedial planning to address deficiencies. Public charter schools are held to the state regulations developed to be in compliance with NCLB. This means that school results are publicized, and parents are notified of low-performing schools and schools that are persistently violent. However, unlike in traditional public schools, where parents don't typically have a choice as to which school their child attends, parents of charter school students can transfer their children out of a charter school at any time. In a traditional public school, parents are provided that option only when the school is designated as low performing.

Option to turn low-performing schools into charter schools. Under the NCLB Act, one of the restructuring models for turning around a low-performing school is to reopen the school as a public charter school. In employing this turnaround option, the failing school would close and reopen with new structures for instructional program, finance and governance. The school would operate independently of the district and would follow accountability measures as defined in its state legislation. This option would be employed after various other restructuring methods had failed to help the school meet AYP goals, and the school is continuing to do so for five consecutive years. If done sagely, the school would utilize appropriate data to identify roadblocks to success that could not be overcome as part of the traditional public school district and make the necessary changes to avoid those roadblocks as part of the charter school authorization application.

It must be noted that state legislation sets the parameters for how a low-performing school will be reopened as a charter school. In some states, the local school board or district is considered a charter school authorizer. If a state has multiple authorizers of charter schools, the choice of authorizer in the case of reopening a school as a public charter school is of paramount concern to the success of the school. Using the model of a district chartering a school in order to reopen it as a public charter school, a specific protocol for the chartering must be in place to ensure success. It would be assumed that it was with district support that the restructuring plan would have been in place for the five years that the school had not met AYP targets. So the plan for reopening the school under public charter status would have to approach support and accountability in ways that are very different from the current manner in which the district holds schools accountable and supports them.

Race to the Top competitive funds

In 2009, President Obama authorized the American Recovery and Reinvestment Act. The Act provided $4.35 billion for the **Race to the Top fund**. This fund is "a competitive grant program designed to encourage and reward States that are creating the conditions for education innovation and reform; achieving significant improvement in student outcomes, including making substantial gains in student achievement, closing achievement gaps, improving high school graduation rates, and ensuring student preparation for success in college and careers; and implementing ambitious plans in four core education reform areas:

Race to the Top fund

A competitive funding program sponsored by the U.S. Department of Education to encourage reforms to state education programs.

+ Adopting standards and assessments that prepare students to succeed in college and the workplace and to compete in the global economy;
+ Building data systems that measure student growth and success, and inform teachers and principals about how they can improve instruction;
+ Recruiting, developing, rewarding, and retaining effective teachers and principals, especially where they are needed most; and
+ Turning around our lowest-achieving schools. (Race to the Top Program Executive Summary, U.S. Department of Education, 2009)

Additionally, the Race to the Top competitive funding is awarded to states that commit to turning around the lowest achieving schools in the following ways—through a turnaround model, a restart model, school closure or a transformation model.

The competitive grant application was worth 500 points. Forty of those points were given for the section *(F) (2) Ensuring successful conditions for high-performing charter schools and other innovative schools.* This section was rated on the following criteria:

(F)(2) Ensuring successful conditions for high-performing charter schools and other innovative schools (40 points)

The extent to which—

(i) The State has a charter school law that does not prohibit or effectively inhibit increasing the number of high-performing charter schools (as defined in this notice) in the State, measured (as set forth in Appendix B) by the percentage of total schools in the State that are allowed to be charter schools or otherwise restrict student enrollment in charter schools;

(ii) The State has laws, statutes, regulations, or guidelines regarding how charter school authorizers approve, monitor, hold accountable, reauthorize, and close charter schools; in particular, whether authorizers require that student achievement (as defined in this notice) be one significant factor, among others, in authorization or renewal; encourage charter schools that serve student populations that are similar to local district student populations, especially relative to high-need students (as defined in this notice); and have closed or not renewed ineffective charter schools;

(iii) The State's charter schools receive (as set forth in Appendix B) equitable funding compared to traditional public schools, and a commensurate share of local, State, and Federal revenues;

(iv) The State provides charter schools with funding for facilities (for leasing facilities, purchasing facilities, or making tenant improvements), assistance with facilities acquisition, access to public facilities, the ability to share in bonds and mill levies, or other supports; and the extent to which the State does not impose any facility-related requirements on charter schools that are stricter than those applied to traditional public schools; and

(v) The State enables LEAs to operate innovative, autonomous public schools (as defined in this notice) other than charter schools.

While 40 out of 500 points may seem like a minimal appropriation of competitive points in a state's grant application, there was strong support for charter schools within the Race to the Top funding program.

Education Secretary Arne Duncan stated the emphasis on charter school legislation and the awarding of Race to the Top funds, telling reporters in a conference call:

"States that do not have public charter laws or put artificial caps on the growth of charter schools will jeopardize their applications under the Race to the Top Fund," Secretary Duncan said. "To be clear, this administration is not looking to open unregulated and unaccountable schools. We want real autonomy for charters combined with a rigorous authorization process and high performance standards." (US DOE website. http://www2.ed.gov/news/pressreleases/2009/06 /06082009a.html. Downloaded 5/31/11)

As of this writing, two rounds of funding for Race to the Top have been distributed through a competitive process. The first two states receiving funding were Tennessee and Delaware. Second round funding was awarded to the District of Columbia, Florida, Georgia, Hawaii, Maryland, Massachusetts, New York, North Carolina, Ohio and Rhode Island.

These states have various records regarding their charter school laws. The following table provides charter school legislation rankings for each of the states as measured by criteria from the Center for Education Reform and the National Alliance for Public Charter Schools. The Center for Education Reform (CER) measures state charter school legislation based on the use of multiple authorizers, the number of schools allowed, school operations and equity. The National Alliance for Public Charter Schools

State receiving Race to the Top funding	CER ranking of state's charter legislation - 2011 (based on score of A, B, C, D, F)	NAPCS ranking of state's charter legislation (score out of 208 possible points and rank among states with charter legislation)
Tennessee	C	90/208 points/Rank: 29
Delaware	C	104/208 points/Rank: 18
District of Columbia	A	123/208 points/Rank: 8
Florida	B	135/208 points/Rank: 2
Georgia	C	126/208 points/Rank: 7
Hawaii	D	74/208 points/Rank: 31
Maryland	D	39/208 points/Rank: 40
Massachusetts	C	132/208 points/Rank: 3
New York	B	129/208 points/Rank: 5
North Carolina	D	76/208 points/Rank: 32
Ohio	C	95/208 points/Rank: 27
Rhode Island	D	64/208 points/Rank: 37

(NAPCS) measures the efficacy of state legislation based on 20 components of their model charter school law. Each of these evaluation methods is described in chapter three of this primer.

As we can see from these rankings, quality of charter legislation was not necessarily a key factor in the awarding of the competitive grant funds. The Center for Education Reform found only one of the Race to the Top recipients worthy of a grade of A. There were 2 B's, 5 C's and 4 D's as well. And while Florida, which ranks as having the second best charter school legislation among chartering states, was awarded Race to the Top funding, some states ranking as low as 32/40, 37/40 and 40/40 when compared to a model charter school law, were also awarded funding.

While the public perception of Race to the Top competitive funding seems to be that the money is focused on charter school development, actual awards of the funds are based on far more criteria than quality of charter school legislation.

Growth of the Movement

National data from the 2009–10 school year shows that there are 4,919 public charter schools in the United States. That is about 5% of all public schools. (There are 91,391 non-charter public schools in this same school year.) Of the 4,919 public charter schools, the average number of years they have been open is 6.7 years. Twenty-seven percent are new, having been open for only 1-3 years. Twenty-six percent have been open for 4–6 years, 19% for 7–9 years and 28% have been open for 10 or more years.

During the 2009–10 school year, 443 new charter schools were opened and 160 closed. The largest concentration of charter schools is at the elementary school level. Forty-three percent of charter schools are at the elementary grades, 10% at the middle school grades, 21% are high schools, 11% are combination middle/high schools and 11% are elementary through high school. There are also 219 ungraded charter schools in the U.S. (Data from the National Alliance of Public Charter Schools website, http://dashboard.publiccharters.org/dashboard/schools/year/2010, retrieved 6/2/2011.)

As the data above show, 160 charter schools were closed during the 2009-10 school year. The movement continues to grow, with new schools opening at a rate that exceeds the number closing. Charter advocates would argue that closing of charter schools really does, in a convoluted way, strengthen the growth of the public charter school movement. In their chapter in Accountability in Action—A Comprehensive Guide to Charter School Closure, Peyser and Marino (2010) point to three reasons that charter school closing is a necessary thing. Closing bad charter school is important for (1) safeguarding students and parents from schools that fail to meet basic standards; (2) creating leverage for broader reform by raising the bar; and (3) protecting the public interest from poor governance or mismanagement. The promise of decreased mandates for stronger accountability must be followed through on, and by keeping this promise, charter school authorizers uphold their dedication to the creation of high-quality public charter schools.

Summary of the History and Growth of the Public Charter School Movement

The creation of public charter schools emanated from a variety of reforms focused on making decisions about education for children closer to the source—at the school level, instead of at the district or state level. The initial iterations of legislation around charter schools were based on the idea that teachers would be able to create their own school models, run their own schools and be held accountable for student outcomes. Eventually state legislation evolved to support education service providers for charter schools, bringing a for-profit motivation to public education.

Public charter school legislation is enacted at the state level. While some generalizations can be made regarding charter legislation, most state legislation varies substantially. At the federal level, charter schools has been supported in various federal level acts, and competitive funding has been made available to support charter schools.

The movement continues to grow at rates that far exceed the closures inherent in a system with high levels of accountability. Forty states and the District of Columbia have public charter school legislation. Approximately 5% of public schools in the country are public charter schools. True authorizer accountability procedures base public charter school renewals and closings on multiple forms of data collected regarding academic performance, fiscal stability and school governance.

GLOSSARY

Magnet schools—Magnet schools are public schools of choice. They can be at the elementary or high school level. Magnet schools develop a theme-based program to attract students to attend the school. An overarching goal of the magnet school philosophy is to end desegregation by drawing a diverse student body to the school.

Small Schools Project—The Small Schools Project is an initiative to create smaller learning communities in public schools. Some small schools are created within a single small community of learners, others are larger schools that are created around various themes and housed in the same building. Commonalities in small schools are small, theme-based learning communities and the nurturing of strong adult-student relationships.

School-based decision-making—A process by which teams of stakeholders make decisions about instructional program, budgeting, professional development and other school-related issues at the school level, rather than at the district level.

Site-based management—Another term for school-based decision-making, where teams of stakeholders make decisions about instructional program, budgeting, professional development and other school-related issues at the school level, rather than at the district level

Decentralized decision-making—The distribution of decision-making power throughout a group or organization, instead of focused at the top of the organization. Typically accountability for the decentralized decisions made is also distributed.

Albert Shanker (1928–1997)—A civil rights activist, union leader, and vocal proponent of education reform, Albert Shanker was elected as president of the American Federation of Teachers (AFT) in 1974. The concept of the creation of charter schools is often attributed to Mr. Shanker, but in fact he simply supported an idea for teacher power in education as presented in a paper by Ray Budd in 1988.

Citizens League of Minneapolis, Minnesota—A group created to build "civic infrastructure" by framing policy problems,

developing civic leaders and building relationships to achieve their goals.

Outcome-based schools—Schools created by Minnesota Law, Chapter 265, Article 9, Section 3. [120.064], the first state charter school legislation. These schools were to be created by teachers with the assistance of advisory boards. Outcome-based schools in Minnesota were the first public charter schools.

Educational Management Organizations—Organizations that assist in the creation and management of public charter schools. These organizations can be non-profit or for-profit organizations.

Educational Service Providers—Organizations that provide contracted services to public charter schools. These organizations can be non-profit or for-profit.

Elementary and Secondary Act (ESEA)—A law initially passed in 1965 and reauthorized every five years. The original purpose of ESEA was to improve educational opportunities for poor children.

Charter School Expansion Act of 1998—An amendment of Titles VI and X of ESEA 1965 to improve and expand charter schools.

No Child Left Behind (NCLB) Act—A reauthorization of the 1965 ESEA. This Act of 2001, signed into law by President Bush in January 2002, changed the landscape of education by holding states accountable for academic progress of all students as measured by a school's adequate yearly progress. Schools failing to make such progress were sanctioned under this Act.

Race to the Top fund—A competitive funding program sponsored by the U.S. Department of Education to encourage reforms to state education programs.

CHAPTER THREE

Legislation and Politics

Overview of the Chapter

In this chapter, we will look at the legislation and politics that influence charter schools. We will examine state legislation that governs charter school authorization and implementation. Funding formulas for charter schools, which vary by state, will also be a topic of discussion. We will look at how states authorize charter schools, and who has the power of authorization and oversight of charter schools. In this discussion we will also examine the idea of local districts as charter school authorizers. We will then try to sort out the politics of charter schools by looking at the stakeholders who are involved in education and how the charter school movement has influenced their advocacy efforts.

Legislation at the State Level

The importance of the quality of state charter school legislation cannot be overstated. Strong charter school legislation equates to strong authorization requirements, high-quality oversight and solid, trained governance. Because states are continually reauthorizing or amending charter school law, inclusion of individual state charter school legislation data will not be discussed here. Rather, we will focus on the work of various charter school advocacy groups that have defined ideal charter school legislation. They define these ideals based on aspects of legislation that give charter schools the most freedom to operate in a way that meets the needs of children, while holding the school accountable for student learning and progress. These organizations not only define the ideal charter school legislation, but also analyze state law based on a comparison to their ideal.

The Center for Education Reform (CER), a charter-friendly school reform 501c3 public, non-profit organization in the District of Columbia conducted audits of state charter school legislation. The criteria CER uses for evaluating state charter school legislation and practice include data based on the legislation's use of multiple authorizers, the number of schools allowed, operations and equity. They grade legislation in each area.

States scoring high in the **Multiple Authorizer** category would mean that the legislation moves authorization responsibility beyond local school boards for authorization and management. High scoring state legislation in this area would allow universities, uniquely created state agencies, non-profit organizations and mayors to authorize and create management structures for charter schools.

States scoring high in the Number of Schools Allowed category may seem self-explanatory. In some states, **charter school caps** are placed on the legal limit of charter schools a state is allowed to have. However, the organization also examines other limits that the states' legislation my put on charter school numbers, like having no cap, but limiting enrollment by school or grade, or restricting funding of the schools.

When examining Operations, CER looks at how schools are allowed to operate per the legislation. Freedom to operate a school as needed, free from bureaucratically dictated procedures is given a higher ranking by CER. Additionally, CER places high value on state legislation that provides charter schools with freedom from collective bargaining.

The Equity category is based on the amount and method of funding charter school students. In this category, CER rates more favorably legislation in which public charter school students are funded with the same amount

---

Multiple Authorizers

Provide charter applicants with a choice of organizations to work with in the charter authorization process. May include universities, uniquely created state agencies, non-profit organizations, mayors and local districts to authorize and create management structures for charter schools

---

Charter school caps

State limits placed on the number of charter schools that can be authorized.

of money, and in the same manner, as traditional public school students.

This organization sees these conditions of charter school legislation as strong indicators of the creation of public charter schools that are capable of providing outstanding educational experiences for students.

The National Alliance for Public Charter Schools also monitors state legislation and compares it against a "model charter school law." This model law outlines 20 components of a model law: These essential components of a strong public charter school law were created by Louann Bierlein Palmer, Associate Professor at Western Michigan University. (Palmer also developed the original list of essential components of a strong public charter school law while she was at the Morrison Institute at Arizona State University during the early 1990s.)

1. No Caps—States are judged on whether their charter school legislation limits the number of public charter schools or students. If caps on school creation or student enrollment exist, legislation is judged favorably if it provides adequate room for growth.

2. A Variety of Public Charter Schools Allowed—States ranked most favorably on this indicator allow a variety of charter schools including new **start-up charter schools, public school conversions** and/or **virtual charter schools**.

Start-up charters

A school that is chartered as a new school, as opposed to a charter school that is converted from an existing public school.

Public school conversions/conversion charter school

A traditional public school that is approved to become an independently operated public charter school.

Virtual charter schools

A school in which teachers and students interact via electronic media.

3. Multiple Authorizers Available—State legislation that allows authorization from two or more viable authorizing agencies, with each having the ability to accept applications directly from applicants are looked upon more favorably than states with only one route to authorization.

4. Authorizer Accountability System Required— Authorizer accountability is a more complex notion. The model charter school law looks for accountability to include an application process for potential authorizers; submission of an annual report summarizing activities of authorizer and performance of schools; regular reviews of authorizers, with accountability measures in place to assure high-quality authorization; review and evaluation of state charter school programs and outcomes.

5. Adequate Authorizer Funding—States need to guarantee adequate funding of authorizers and require public reporting of expenditures in order to receive a favorable rating in this category. Other indicators of adequate funding for authorizers include that authorizers must have a separate contract for the purchase of authorizer services by charter schools and the state legislation must prohibit authorizers from requiring that schools purchase services from the authorizer.

6. Transparent Charter Application, Review and Decision-Making Processes—Ideally, state legislation would include transparency assurances regarding the application elements for all schools; additional issues related to conversion schools and virtual schools; specifications for application when using educational service providers or replication models. Legislation should also include requirements for authorizer-issued requests for proposals and thorough evaluations of all applications. Chartering decisions should be made in public meetings and provide feedback regarding any denial decisions.

7. Performance-Based Charter Contracts Required—A model charter school law would assure that **performance-based charter contracts** were in place to define the roles, power and responsibilities of the school and its authorizer. Certain academic and operational performance expectations need to be defined and include academic indicators, financial indicators and board stewardship and compliance indicators. Terms of charters under a model charter school law would be five or more years with periodic reviews.

8. Comprehensive Public Charter School Monitoring and Data Collection Processes—States ranking high on this category have monitoring and data collection processes that include measures of student outcome data and financial accountability. Such legislation would enable authorizers to conduct oversight activities and make annual school performance reports public. Additionally, such legislation should direct authorizers to notify schools of perceived problems and take appropriate corrective actions steps to remediate the problem.

9. Clear Processes for Renewal, Nonrenewal, and Revocation Decisions—The model charter school

---

Charter school performance contract

A legally binding agreement between a charter school authorizer and a charter school that delineates the rights and responsibilities of each.

legislation should not only support clear processes, but also clear criteria for renewal, nonrenewal and revocation of a charter. This aspect of the law should also provide for due process, timely notification, public meetings, responses in writing, authority to vary length of charter renewal, and provisions for smooth transition of students and records.

10. Educational Service Providers Allowed—Ideal charter school legislation would allow all types of service providers, requiring evidence of past success in the educational arena. Contracts would be required between charter school boards and educational service providers, and conflicts of interest would be required to be disclosed in the charter application.

11. Fiscally and Legally Autonomous Schools, with Independent Public Charter School Boards—States scoring high on this indicator have legislation that assures that schools are both fiscally and legally autonomous, with governing boards created specifically for the purpose of governing charter schools.

12. Clear Student Recruitment, Enrollment and Lottery Procedures—The model charter school law calls for state legislation to support open enrollment; lottery requirements; enrollment preferences for previously enrolled students in conversions, prior year students in chartered and siblings of enrolled students, as well as limits of 10% of school population on any optional enrollments of children of school founders, governing board members and full-time employees.

13. Automatic Exemptions from Many State and District Laws and Regulations—Model charter school law would exempt charter schools from teacher certification and any other laws EXCEPT those covering health, safety, civil rights, student accountability, employee criminal history checks, open meetings, freedom of information, and generally accepted accounting principles.

14. Automatic Collective Bargaining Exemption—States scoring high in this category have legislation that supports exemption of participation in district collective bargaining agreements. This includes charter schools authorized by local or non-local boards authorizers.

15. Multi-School Charter Contracts and Multi-Charter Contract Boards Allowed—State legislation inclusive

of this aspect of charter school law would allow charter school boards to oversee multiple schools, either
through a linked single contract, or a single contract
agreement for each school.

16. Extra-Curricular and Interscholastic Activities
Eligibility and Access—Model charter school legislation includes this provision for state law to include
charter school students and employees as eligible to
participate in all interscholastic leagues, competitions,
awards, scholarship and recognition programs as non-
charter public school students. If charter schools cannot provide such opportunities, the law should state
that charter schools have access to those activities at
non-charter public schools for a fee mutually agreed
upon.

17. Clear Identification of Special Education Responsibilities—This clarification in the model charter school
law includes clarity in the law regarding which entity is
the **LEA (Local Education Agency)** responsible for providing special education services and clarity regarding
funding for low-incident, high-cost services for charter schools in the same amount and manner to other
LEAs.

**Local Education Agency
(LEA)**

A legal term that defines
a public school board
whose responsibilities
include running the
school or district, taking
responsibility for
compliance with
mandates, contracting for
services and receiving
grant money.

18. Equitable Operational Funding and Equal Access to
All State and Federal Categorical Funding—States
scoring high in this category assure equitable operational funding as per state statute, equal access to all
applicable categorical federal and state funding, and
clear guidance on pass-through funding. Additionally,
a model charter school law would provide funding for
transportation similar to school districts.

19. Equitable Access to Capital Funding and Facilities—
Model charter school legislation calls for per pupil
facilities allowances which reflect annual actual
average district capital costs; state grants for charter
school facilities; equal access to tax-exempt bonding
authorities or allowing charter schools to have their
own bonding authority; credit enhancement for public
charter school facilities; equal access to existing state
facilities programs available to non-charter public
schools; right of first refusal to purchase or lease at or
below fair market value a closed, unused, or underused
public school facility or property; prohibition of facil-

ity-related requirements stricter than those applied to traditional public schools.

20. Access to Relevant Employee Retirement Systems— An ideal charter school law would allow charter schools to have access to relevant state retirement systems available to other public schools, and have the option to participate in these systems.

The National Alliance for Public Charter Schools analyzes individual state charter schools laws against these model components. Results made public through the State Charter School Rankings Database on the National Alliance for Public Charter Schools website. As states reauthorize their charter school legislation, such rankings provide a benchmark against which they can measure their legislation and balance their charter school programs.

Charter School Funding

Charter school funding is state specific. Charter legislation sets the guidelines for the funding of these schools. Since charter schools are public schools, they cannot charge tuition. Their money comes from state and federal education funding. The charter school funding formulas are typically developed in per pupil dollars. That means a rate is set for each student in charter schools and the charter school gets the per pupil funding to run their school based on the number of students in their school. In most states, public charter schools receive less money per pupil than the traditional public schools in that state. This inequity in funding is of great concern to many stakeholders.

A 2005 study done by the Thomas B. Fordham Institute analyzed charter school funding in states. The study— Charter School Funding: Inequity's Next Frontier—investigated funding from the 2002-03 school year and organized the funding disparities between charter school and district school revenue into four bands. The bands are defined by the percent gap between charter school and district school funding. The first band was favorable, with no more than a 5% gap between charter and district funding. The second band included funding gaps of 5%–14.9%. The third band had larger funding gaps, in the range of 15%–24.9%. And the fourth band schools studied showed a severe inequity between charters and district schools, in the range of 25% or greater. When looking at these variances, the researchers found that two states had funding approaching parity (band one), four states had moderate differences between charter and district school funding (band two), five states had large difference in funding (band three), and six states had what is defined as severe differences in funding (band four). On average, public charter schools received 21.7% less funding than their traditional public school counterparts.

When looking at large urban school district funding rates, and comparing those rates to charter schools located within that geographic area, the gap was even wider. Only one large urban district had charter schools within the geographic area that were approaching funding parity with the public schools (band one). Four had moderate discrepancies (band two). Nine had large discrepancies (band three). And thirteen had severe discrepancies (band four). The average charter school located within the same geographic area as a traditional large urban public school district received 23.5% less funding than their traditional public school counterparts.

In addition to less per pupil aid, charter schools in most states are also not eligible for facilities funding. Traditional public schools are eligible for aid that can be used for the construction and maintenance of buildings. Traditional public schools also have increased borrowing opportunities for funding of projects. Not only don't charter schools receive facilities funding, but they also are typically only chartered for five years at a time, making borrowing funds for a facility difficult.

Charter schools are eligible for federal entitlement money and other federal categorical funds. State and federal grants are also available to help charter schools as they are in their start-up year prior to actually opening the doors of the school. Without such grants, charter schools would not be able to open and purchase necessary equipment and supplies until their students were actually enrolled in the school and the school was receiving their per pupil funding. These grants help with that transition from when the charter is granted to when the school actually begins operation.

The funding inequity is real. Traditional school districts would argue that they need more funds than charter schools because they do not realize a general cost savings when their students leave the district to attend a charter school. In a large urban district, for example, one hundred second graders may leave the district to attend charters.

Those one hundred second graders don't necessarily come from one school. They come from many schools. Therefore the district cannot close a school based on these students leaving. Chances are that they cannot even consolidate second grade classrooms if only a few students are leaving each school. Cost savings are difficult to realize because the overall savings to a district with only a small percentage of students leaving to go to charter schools are minimal. The school must still operate school buildings, employ central office staff, and pay teacher salaries. Some would argue that the excess in per pupil funding that the traditional public school districts receive is justified to maintain the overall district costs that are not decreased when students leave the district to enroll in charter schools.

Funding is key to implementation of educational programs. The distribution of funds to educate students in schools is an important indicator of the value we place on the education of the students. It is important to provide adequate funding to ensure that public charter school students receive appropriate supports and that traditional public schools can also continue to support student learning.

Charter School Authorizers

High quality charter schools are dependent on high-quality authorization protocol. Charter school authorizers are the organizations that are empowered to grant schools charters, to hold charter schools that they authorize accountable, to regularly evaluate the schools they authorize, and to renew—or revoke—charters based on the schools' performance.

Charter school authorization varies by state and is defined in individual state legislation. As mentioned earlier in this chapter, model charter school law, as defined by the National Alliance for Public Charter Schools, highly rates state charter school legislation that assures that there are multiple charter school authorizers in the state, that the authorizers are held accountable, and that the authorizers are adequately funded.

The number of authorizers in states varies greatly. In some states, there is only one authorizer empowered to charter schools. Some states have multiple authorizers. California currently has over 200 authorizers. In most cases of a state using single authorizer, the authorizer is a state education agency. Authorizers can also be local education agencies (school districts or school boards), independent chartering boards, higher education institutions, municipalities or not-for-profit organization.

The National Association of Charter School Authorizers (NACSA) has published a guidebook of standards for high-quality charter school authorizing. They base their standards on three core principles of charter authorizing—maintaining high standards for schools, upholding school autonomy, and protecting student and public interests. The organizations standards include:

+ Agency Commitment and Capacity: A quality authorizer recognizes that chartering is a means to foster excellent schools that meet identified needs; clearly prioritizes a commitment to excellence in education and in authorizing practices; and creates organizational structures and commits human and financial resources necessary to conduct its authorizing duties effectively and efficiently.

+ Application Process and Decision Making: A quality authorizer implements a comprehensive application process that includes clear application questions and guidance; follows fair, transparent procedures and rigorous criteria; and grants charters only to applicants who demonstrate a strong capacity to establish and operate a quality charter school

+ Performance Contracting: A quality authorizer executes contracts with charter schools that articulate the rights and responsibilities of each party regarding school autonomy, funding, administration and oversight, outcomes, measures for evaluating success or failure, performance consequences, and other material terms. The contract is an essential document, separate from the charter application, which establishes the legally binding agreement and terms under which the school will operate.

+ Ongoing Oversight and Evaluation: A quality authorizer conducts contract oversight that competently evaluates performance and monitors compliance; ensures schools' legally entitled autonomy; protects student rights; informs intervention, revocation, and renewal decisions; and provides annual public reports on school performance.

+ Revocation and Renewal Decision Making: A quality authorizer designs and implements a transparent and rigorous process that uses comprehensive academic, financial, and operational performance data to make merit-based renewal decisions, and revokes charters when necessary to protect student and public interests.

These standards serve as a basis for the creation of authorization processes that will result in high-quality public charter school choices for children in the United States.

School Districts as Charter School Authorizers

Perhaps this is a perfect segue to discussion of school districts as charter school authorizers. The Center for Comprehensive School Reform and Improvement has studied models of district "chartering" of their own schools and report that various factors need to be in place for this to be a successful experience. The study finds that there are five main factors that need to be addressed: (1) System-level governance; (2) Environmental factors; (3) School-level governance; (4) Leadership factors; and (5) Organizational factors (Center for Comprehensive School Reform, Reopening as a Charter School, 2005).

System-level governance refers to the district as charter authorizer and overseer. Here the district needs to ensure that the application that is created for the low-performing school that will be reopened as a charter is rigorous and ensures that the school personnel and founders will be able to carry out the program as described. Because the school will be reopening as an independently operated public school, the decision about the school program must include confidence that not only is the academic program sound, but also that the organizational structure will appropriately sustain the program. Legal and financial considerations must also be taken into account to assure success on all levels of accountability.

In order to accomplish this level of oversight and authority, a school district would need to have appropriate resources to staff such an accountability office with experts to carry out the tasks as required. The office that would oversee the district-chartered school(s) would need to have the capacity to create an environment for charter school

success. The study suggests that districts could successfully outsource this authorizing and oversight responsibility to an organization that already has the capacity and
reputation for strong authorization and oversight, thereby
relieving the district of creating protocol for this new role.

Environmental factors. The study also indicates that there
are many environmental factors, or factors outside of the
charter's control, that need to be in place for a charter
school to be successful. Issues of level of autonomy, expectations of accountability, time necessary for restructuring,
and additional support (funding, facilities, technical assistance and training) must be constructed in a way that will
lead the charter school to have an environment created in
which the school and the students are poised for success.

School-level governance. This is key to the success of any
public charter school, and is also key to schools being
reopened as charter schools through NCLB restructuring. Boards that govern charter schools need to have a clear
vision for the school. They need to understand their role
as board members. As such, they need to have the capacity to hire a strong leader and develop strategic plans and
policies to lead the school to success. While a school that
is closed and reopened as a charter school may retain some
of its original identity, the school-level governance structure is most likely a new construct that must be carefully
crafted for success.

Leadership factors. These also play a large role in the success of any school or organization. Leaders in charter
schools play a different role than leaders in traditional
public schools (see chapter 4 for a detailed discussion of
the role of the charter school leader). Such leaders need
to be results-driven, confident problem solvers who know
how to influence others. They need to be committed to
the school and ready to lead based on the needs and goals
of the school. School leaders must be carefully chosen,
trained, evaluated and retained for them to successfully
lead a public charter school.

Organizational factors. Factors such as school program
and staff development must be considered in setting up a
reopened school for success. The report has found that the
ability to select teachers for a reopened school is an impor-

tant consideration. Teachers need to not only believe in the new mission of the school, but also must be able to teach in alignment with that mission. Those are two qualities that are not always found together. A teacher may "believe" that it is important for a school to have a technology focus to prepare students for a myriad of career paths in the tech industry. However, the same teacher may not have the technology skills, the desire to pursue those skills, or the forethought to present concepts that would lead students to develop those skills. Having a passion for the belief and having the skill to deliver the content are not the same, so hiring and developing a new teaching staff that can deliver the instruction required in the school program is important.

Additionally, the new school may have a new school culture. Expectations of employees and students and parents and community members may be different than when the school was a traditional public school. It will be important for those working at the school to be able to work in that culture, and not work counter to the culture.

Careful attention must be paid to the development of the school program. Many research-based and practice-based criteria for success of public charter schools have been studied. These include approaches to behavior management, curriculum, parental involvement, uninterrupted instructional time, high-quality formative and summative assessment, and flexibility to carry out the school's mission. These issues must be in place and supported to set the school up for success.

When failing traditional public schools reopen as charters, it is important to realize that the conditions that led the school to be low performing must be addressed within the new model. The charter model is not a panacea in and of itself. The model succeeds when it is carefully planned, authorized and monitored. This report gives guidance for such tenets of success.

P(p)olitics of Charter Schools

There are various stakeholders in education. These are people who are interested in high-quality education and work as a group to strive for increased student learning and achievement. They are groups that act and may advocate for reforms and policies that they feel will benefit the educational system the most. Each comes at educational reform from a unique perspective. We will look at each of these stakeholder groups in this section, describing who they are, what position they take in the education reform arena, and how the charter school movement has impacted their message.

Parents as Stakeholders

We'll begin by looking at parents as a stakeholder group. When one looks objectively at the group, it is obvious that they may have the most at stake—the education and future success of their children. Parents cover a wide range of stakeholders, however. Upper- and middle-class parents typically live in areas where school taxes are high, schools provide many opportunities for students, and when disappointed with a school system, these parents have the means by which to move to a home in a different school district, lobby the district for changes, or send their children to tuition-driven private schools. Parents who are struggling financially don't have those educational options available for their children. If they are stuck in a failing school district, there is little choice to move from those failing schools. Private school tuition may be prohibitive. And moving to a district where schools are of higher quality may be unaffordable. So while all parents want high-quality education for their students, differences in financial means divides parents on the ability to provide such opportunities.

Parents have traditionally played a supportive role in schools. They participated in fund-raising events, volunteered in classrooms, led after-school activities. The National PTA has a long history of working to advocate for reforms in schools. Such reforms include mandating sprinklers, as well as fire escapes, in schools; advocating for hot lunch programs; and encouraging the enacting of Goals 2000. Parent groups continue to learn more about their rights, especially when their children attend failing schools. California's Parent Trigger Law empowers parents in chronically underperforming schools to petition their school board to make sweeping changes. Parents in these schools can sign a petition. Fifty percent plus one signatures can lead to required restructuring of a school by the school board. The school can be restructured, shut down, all staff can be fired, or the school can be converted to a charter school. The California Parent Trigger Law gives parents the right to demand reform.

The charter school movement has led to increased activism among parents. Charter schooling as a public school choice option means that parents who previously were prisoners of a failing school system have a choice. Parents can pursue school choice options, independent of the school system, through enrollment in an existing charter school. Parents who are looking for school choice options that are not available can join founding groups to open charter schools that will better meet the need of the community. Many states require parent satisfaction surveys as a part of a charter school's annual reporting. And the inherent parent satisfaction tool of keeping a child enrolled in a school—and thereby keeping the school viable—is really the ultimate satisfaction instrument in charter schools.

Teachers as Stakeholders

Teachers are an obvious stakeholder group in education. Note that we will discuss teachers as stakeholders in this section. A specific section about teacher unions as stakeholders will follow.

People enter the profession of teaching because they care deeply about student learning. Traditional teacher preparation programs encourage lesson creativity, meaningful instruction, and alignment to standards. Teachers learn how to manage classrooms, interact with parents, and assess students. They eagerly volunteer to direct school plays and coach the seventh grade cheerleading squad. They can often be seen taking bags filled with papers home to be graded over the weekend. They create materials to enhance learning in the classroom.

When we look at the majority of teachers and their role in education reform, we see a reform movement that is much closer to the ground than others. Teachers think of reform and how it effects their students. They are so busy worrying about the main outcome of education—student learning—that they don't focus on the larger educational restructuring efforts that take place in other arenas. Teacher reform efforts are more focused on instructional reform. They look at new learning theories and how those theories can impact student success in their classroom. Their professional development is focused on teaching strategy or assessment strategy. Perhaps they are looking at the reforms that can take place in student learning when students have access to technology. They look for ways to help students.

The larger reform efforts that come about in the local, state or federal educational systems may impact what happens in the classroom, but typical teachers are too busy working in those classrooms to worry about the larger educational structure. They may rely on their unions to inform them of changes and to lobby on their behalf.

This is rather ironic, because teachers are typically the target of many of the larger reform issues. Changes in teacher certification requirements, mandated professional development hours, federally approved research-based programs, and professional evaluations based on student results are all reform-based mandates that affect teachers. Teachers follow those mandates as directed by their building leaders, who are most likely directed by district leaders, to follow those mandates. Teachers may turn to their unions for support in these mandates, but for the most part, take them in stride and continue to work toward increasing student learning.

Teachers are involved in reforms in traditional schools at various levels. They may serve on site-based management teams, or various school committees that inform teaching and assessment. But they are not necessarily involved in the actual running of the school program.

The charter school movement has changed the activism potential of teachers in significant ways. Keep in mind that Ray Budde and Albert Shanker first conceived of the idea of charter schools as teacher run cooperatives that would give teacher control of instruction and student learning opportunities. Some charter schools are actually true to this initial intent. Teacher cooperatives exist in which teachers have taken control of chartered schools and share the administrative roles in those schools. Other teachers have started their own charter schools, or been on founding boards of schools. This is a significant change in the power of teachers in the educational system. Teachers who choose to work in charter schools also have some instructional advocacy "power." A problem in traditional systems is that mandates make the use of various learning programs and techniques required, with little regard for the input of those closest to student learning, the teacher. In a charter school, there is relief from many of the mandates governing required instructional programs. Instead, teachers and school leaders and other interested stakeholders can tailor programs and instruction to meet the needs of students. This ability to be innovative in an educational setting is a benefit to charter school teachers and empowers them to meet the needs of their students.

Teacher Unions as Stakeholders

Teacher unions have a long history of advocating for the rights of educators and children. They have worked for better conditions for teaching and learning since 1857. Considered by many in the public to be working solely for increased wages for teachers, teacher unions play a much broader role in education reform.

The mission, vision, and core values of the National Education Association, as adopted at the 2006 NEA Representative Assembly are:

Our Vision
Our vision is a great public school for every student.

Our Mission
Our mission is to advocate for education professionals and to unite our members and the nation to fulfill the promise of public education to prepare every student to succeed in a diverse and interdependent world.

Our Core Values
These principles guide our work and define our mission:

Equal Opportunity. We believe public education is the gateway to opportunity. All students have the human and civil right to a quality public education that develops their potential, independence, and character.

A Just Society. We believe public education is vital to building respect for the worth, dignity, and equality of every individual in our diverse society.

Democracy. We believe public education is the cornerstone of our republic. Public education provides individuals with the skills to be involved, informed, and engaged in our representative democracy.

Professionalism. We believe that the expertise and judgment of education professionals are critical to student success. We maintain the highest professional standards, and we expect the status, compensation, and respect due all professionals.

Partnership. We believe partnerships with parents, families, communities, and other stakeholders are essential to quality public education and student success.

Collective Action. We believe individuals are strengthened when they work together for the common good. As education professionals, we improve both our professional status and the quality of public education when we unite and advocate collectively.

NEA also believes every student in America, regardless of family income or place of residence, deserves a quality education. In pursuing its mission, NEA has determined that we will focus the energy and resources of our 3.2 million members on improving the quality of teaching, increasing student achievement and making schools safer, better places to learn. (http://www.nea.org/home/19583. htm, retrieved July 12, 2011)

The NEA works on behalf of its membership to take action on issues like professional pay, education funding, minority community outreach, and dropout prevention. Their work is important and contributes to the education of America's students.

The united voice of the union does not necessarily support charter schools. The NEA supports state affiliates in their positions on charter schools. The NEA's overall position on charter schools is that they have the potential to facilitate educational reform through innovative teaching, which can be replicated in traditional public schools. But they caution that the success of charter schools depends on the design, implementation and oversight of the schools.

The NEA had developed a policy statement regarding state legislation about charter schools. The policy is purposefully broad and relies on individual state affiliates to inform the policy in their states. The NEA's overall policy focuses on several aspects of charter school legislation. They recommend that charters only be granted for programs that are qualitatively different than traditional programs, that local boards should have the authority to grant or deny charters, that funding for charter schools should not divert resources from traditional public schools, that charter schools should be monitored closely and closed for at-risk practices, that private schools and private for-profits should not be allowed to charter a school, and that charter schools should have the same collective bargaining rights as traditional public schools.

These statements of the NEA policy on charter schools seem fair and equitable, focusing, as one would assume, on the education of students and the rights of teachers. Yet teacher union lobbying efforts against charter school initiatives such as higher caps and the creation of new charters continue. This is not without provocation.

Some early efforts at chartering schools were a result of anti-union sentiment. There were feelings that traditional public schools with strong unions were protecting teacher rights, but preventing the progress of student learning. Some charter schools were founded in a direct counter to those perceptions. Some charter schools advocates have been vocal on this issue. And, as discussed earlier in this chapter, national charter school advocacy groups clearly support model charter school legislation that guarantees an automatic exemption for charter school from collective bargaining agreements. While many parallels can be seen between charter advocate and union advocate perspectives on the public charter school movement, it is hard to deny that there is a wide disagreement on the issue of collective bargaining.

In May of 2006, two major players in education research and policy, the National Charter School Research Project (NCSRP) and the Progressive Policy Institute (PPI), called a meeting of union leaders and charter school leaders. The meeting resulted in an agreement that both sides of the table were dedicated to the children their schools were serving. Yet each side stuck to their beliefs. Charter school leader beliefs included pay for performance and the creation of professionally fulfilling work environments. Union leaders worried about teacher respect in charter schools and felt that the development of clear roles, rights and responsibilities would guarantee respect and professionalism. While these don't seem to be conflicting beliefs, the manner in which each side realizes its vision is where the conflict comes to light. The pay for performance and professionally fulfilling work environments advocated by charter school proponents manifest through school environments that traditionally do not include tenure for teachers, and place a high value on teacher creativity, governance and responsibility. Union leaders' beliefs manifest through contractual agreements where the delineation of responsibilities and rights is written and agreed upon my teachers and management.

As with most conflict, it seems that many of the perceptions of the people involved come from anecdotal evidence and narrow experience regarding the other side's experiences. There are obviously many traditional public schools that have very good teacher-leader relationships, with satisfied teachers who are respected professionally. There are also traditional public school teachers who, even with union protections in place, need to create work-to-rule environments because the teachers are being treated unfairly by management and their rights are being violated. The same is true of charter school environments. Some charter schools create respectful and professional working relationships that are based on the importance of teacher input for student success. Other charter schools are more corporate in nature, with corporate mandates replacing bureaucratic mandates. In these charter schools, a more clear emphasis on teacher rights may be in order.

School Boards as Stakeholders

Local boards of education are certainly stakeholders in the educational system. Local board members are elected for specific terms of office and serve to govern and set policy for the school system they represent. Local boards of education can join their state affiliate School Board Association. The National School Board Association (NSBA) represents those state affiliates at a national level.

NSBA's mission is "working with and through our state associations, to advocate for equity and excellence in public education through school board leadership" (http://www.nsba.org/About.aspx. Retrieved July 12, 2011).

This organization has worked to support public education on important issues of education reform. Among the key advocacy issues NSBA is involved with are the reauthorization of the Elementary and Secondary Education Act, federal funding for education, early childhood education, flexibility in academic core standards, and child nutrition.

The organization has developed a position statement on charter schools. The position paper cites challenges that charter schools present to local school districts, especially urban school districts where the majority of charter schools tend to be opened. Its concerns include issues of facilities for charter schools, personnel issues, student enrollment, and the community involvement of charter schools. The official position of the organization regarding charter schools is that charter schools should have to abide by the same environmental, labor, due process and fiscal laws as traditional public schools. They also believe that only local public school systems and elected boards of education should be able to sponsor charter schools, and determine the accountability criteria to be used to judge if they are viable. The local systems and boards would also retain the authority to revoke a charter from a school. Regarding funding, the NSBA believes that the charter schools must be accountable for public funds and that funds of the local district are not diminished by the funding of charter schools.

Community Members as Community Stakeholders

Community members can include business owners, medical professionals, bankers, community service organizations, etc. There are many people who live in and care about communities. In turn, they care about the education of young people in the community. There concern is altruistic in nature—the desire for all children to have access to high-quality, free public education. However, their concern might also go beyond care for the individual. The concern might go to the level of community development—the desire for children to be educated and productive members of society and of the community. The concern might also go to the level of the need for a sustainable community—educated children will make productive workers and keep the community viable. Community members' concerns about education are varied and valid.

Historically, community members were able to participate in the public education system in a few ways. They could meet with the principal of a local school to voice their concerns. Depending on the level of concern, it could be handled at the school level or would be referred to the central administration of the district. Community members could also speak about a concern to their representative on the district's board of education. Additionally they could make their concern known at the public school board meeting. Community members can also run for election to the school board and be a key decision maker in the district. All of these forms of influencing public education are based on working within the traditional system of public education.

The charter school movement gave community stakeholders a new option to influence public education. Instead of trying to influence the traditional system of public education, community stakeholders now had an option to create the schools that would address their issues of concern. They could work with educators to found schools that had unique programs that would provide high-quality education, safe environments, and prepare workers to sustain local professions and businesses. This empowerment of community stakeholders provides a way for communities to stay viable and control their children's educational systems.

Federal and State Departments of Education as Stakeholders

The Departments of Education at the federal and state levels have, as their main concern, the provision of high-quality education for all children. Efforts at providing equitable, high-quality educational opportunities have been at the forefront of these governmental departments for years. Federal initiatives like the Elementary and Secondary Education Act (ESEA), Goals 2000, No Child Left Behind (NCLB) and Race to the Top (RttT) are national initiatives to improve the quality and equity of education for all students. They are based on equal opportunity and access, high standards, assessment and accountability for results. These federal initiatives provide a framework for states to set education policy for their schools.

Federal and state legislation and policies were focused attempts to change the system of education from the inside. Compliance with required mandates was expected for schools and districts to be eligible for various funding sources. Meaningful and intelligent integration of mandates into a program would likely result in increased learning on behalf of students. But simple compliance with no meaningful integration would result in a band aid approach to education reform. Without meaningful planning of mandate compliance activities, the mandates became "one more thing" that "they" (state and federal agencies) are making us do.

Reforming a system from within is often a difficult task. When a system develops a homeostatic ebb and flow, it is difficult to disrupt that rhythm, even if the disruption will eventually produce better results. In such cases, external mandates are only tolerated with the hope that they will eventually expire.

However, the charter school movement gave federal and state Departments of Education new "teeth" in moving their reform agenda forward. Charter schools were a way to approach educational reform from outside of the system. Legislating the chartering of independently operated public schools gave educational reform a clean slate from which to work. Authorization of these schools was key to their success. Authorization of charter schools would provide a clean slate from which to work—thereby avoiding dealing with the homeostatic ebb and flow of traditional, entrenched systems. Charter schools could be held to accountability standards that translated traditional public school mandates into standards of success. Mandates are a way to change systems by imposing requirements for practice that will hopefully produce better results. Charter schools could, instead, be required to focus on the "better results" by being held accountable for results. Mandates would not be required for charter schools because they would initiate their programs with the accountability requirements in mind.

The federal Department of Education took the use of charter schools as a reform model one step further. Initially schools were started to give parents a public school choice. This allowed parents to choose charter schools if they were not satisfied with their traditional school options. Under the NCLB Act, schools that were identified as persistently failing would have options for restructuring. One of those options would be to turn the failing district school into a charter school. If the district could not change the school in a way that led to success and high-quality educational opportunities for students, the change could be made from the outside—removing the school from traditional district control and giving it a unique governing board and opportunity to re-create itself from outside of the system.

This lever has increased opportunities for true school reform outside of the existing, sometimes dysfunctional, district structures.

School District Central Office as Stakeholders

A school district central office, or administrative office, is comprised of various offices that are in charge of running the business of the school district. Depending on the size of the school district and the available funding, the central office can consist of a Superintendent, Curriculum Director and Business Manager, or can be much larger and be comprised of hundreds of employees handling everything from human resources, finance, legal, curriculum, assessment, special education, English language learning, and public relations. Much of their work is done to comply with local, state and federal mandates. They also work to coordinate the efforts and the schools to ease the burden of curriculum development, professional development, purchasing and coordination of programs like special education at the school level. By consolidating these services at a central level, the district also realizes a cost savings through addressing issues common to all schools at a centralized location.

As with any centralized management organization, those working in the central office can become detached from the work in the field. For example, retail stores that are centrally managed by a corporation may find that the decisions made at the central headquarters are not necessarily decisions that are in the best interest of the stores' customers. In that case, shoppers may stop making purchases at the stores and profits may suffer. When the employees and leadership of the central headquarters of the retail store refocus their efforts to meet the needs of customers, the customers will return to shopping in the stores and the stores will once again become profitable.

This can happen in a central office of a school district as well. Central office leaders may become overwhelmed by the demands on the district from the outside. There are the demands of external mandates, of internally created processes, of unions, and of board members. Many of the mandates are driven down to the school level, adding more work to the schools that the central office is supposed to be helping. The external demands placed on the central office sometimes take the focus off those that the central office has been created to serve—the schools, students and families. Typically that type of misdirection is allowed to continue unchecked. Even though schools were failing, families weren't necessarily leaving the district. And if families aren't leaving the district, funding remains in place to support not only the schools, but the central office bureaucracy as well.

One problem encountered with the onset of the development of charter schools is that parents now had a public school choice in their children's education. Parents could opt to leave the district and have their children—and the funding that supports their children's schooling—go to a charter school. Much like the example above of the retail store, decisions made at the headquarters—or central office—may have effected decisions made by the customers at the school.

A district could leverage this opportunity for growth at the central office. A district that finds itself with a large percentage of the local population opting for charter schools could reinvent the central office to be a better service provider. Through better and more strategic services being provided to the district schools, the schools could offer a better product—a more rigorous and high-quality educational program—to entice the customers (parents) back to the school. This improvement of services would not only benefit those parents who decide to come back to the district, but would also benefit those families still in the district.

In this way the charter school movement has the capacity to improve education not only for students and families who choose to attend public charter schools, but also for those who chose to stay in the system.

State Specific Charter Assistance Organizations as Stakeholders

The charter school movement has initiated the development of organizations that exist in states to provide guidance and support to those involved in charter schools. These organizations can exist within state Departments of Education, or can be separate organizations—most typically charter school associations or charter school resource centers—that work in a variety of capacities.

Charter assistance organizations

Organizations that assist charter schools with a variety of aspects of setup and operation.

The work of these **charter assistance organizations** can range from providing help with applications for founding groups looking to start charter schools, to educating the public on charter schools and their role in the educational system. Some state charter school associations lobby or advocate on behalf of charter schools. Others provide leadership in accountability. Still others serve as resources for charter school founders, operators, leaders, parents and authorizers. Resources can include workshops, guidance documents, and general technical assistance.

Obviously these organizations are pro-charter organizations that have been developed to support the growth of a quality charter school movement. Their message is that high-quality charter schools are an important school choice option in our educational environment. Their work is focused on perpetuating and strengthening the movement both on the ground, with the creation and maintenance of high-quality public charter schools, and in the legislature through advocacy and lobbying.

State Charter School Authorizers as Stakeholders

Like charter assistance organizations, charter school authorizers were created due to the onset of the charter school movement. Authorizers are empowered to charter schools based on individual state charter school legislation. They are dedicated to the creation of high-quality, accountable charter schools in their state. Once chartered, a school's authorizer is the agency that holds the school accountable for a variety of components, typically academics, finance and governance. Because of their close relationship with the schools they charter, and the schools to which they deny charters, they see the strengths and weaknesses of the policy surrounding this public school choice option. As such, they are in a perfect position to advise on issues that would strengthen individual state charter legislation to enable authorizing that will result in even higher-quality charter schools.

Higher Education Institutions

Higher education institutions (HEI)—colleges and universities—have long played a role in public school education. Teacher preparation programs train teachers to teach in the public schools system. Leadership preparation programs prepare teaching professionals for careers as educational leaders, both at the principal and central office administration levels. Some colleges and universities even run lab schools, or demonstration schools, in which college faculty and K-12 teachers work together to implement research-based practices in a school environment. These are very important contributions to public schooling.

The charter school movement has changed these practices in some significant ways. Some states identify higher education institutions as charter school authorizers. As such, the HEI may take on new responsibilities in the state in which they are located. These responsibilities include recognizing high-quality educational programs, guiding charter school founders in the application process, reviewing applications, providing feedback to applicants, issuing charters to successful applicants, setting accountability measures for charter schools, monitoring schools it has chartered, and renewing or revoking charters based on performance. This is a significant departure from simple teacher and leader preparation responsibilities of colleges and universities.

Additionally, many state-level charter school laws allow charter schools to hire a certain number of uncertified teachers, and may even allow schools to hire school leaders who do not hold state administrative certification. This leaves open the door for colleges and universities to develop programs for charter school leaders and teachers that are not traditional certification-path programs, but rather focus on the unique skill set necessary for charter school professionals to possess. As described in chapter 4 of this primer, charter school leaders are really operating multimillion dollar non-profit agencies in their schools. As such, the skill set that they need to do this is different than the skill set of a traditionally certified educational administrator. Colleges and universities have the opportunity to retool their programming to meet the educational and professional development needs of these charter school professionals.

As continuous advocates for high-quality educational opportunities, colleges and universities can embrace the charter school movement for the prospect it provides for changing education through authorization and the education of a new generation of education professionals.

Summary of the chapter

In this chapter we examined key issues in the legislation that surrounds charter schools. Charter school legislation, funding, and authorization are state specific. As such, it is difficult to draw conclusions about the efficacy of these aspects of the charter school movement as a national movement. However, in analyzing the content of various aspects of legislation, funding and authorization, trends in high-quality work around charter schools can be identified. Comparing state protocols to these models of legislation, funding and authorization can be helpful for informing policy about charter schools.

We've also discussed key players in charter school advocacy. The charter school movement has an effect on various stakeholders in the educational arena. The general public perception of charter schools is typically based on school performance and instructional program in individual schools. However, there is a wide array of stakeholder groups working on behalf of education at administrative, policy and legislative levels, and the charter school movement has an impact on the work of those stakeholders.

GLOSSARY

Multiple Authorizers—Multiple authorizers for charter schools within a state provide charter applicants with a choice of organizations to work with in the charter authorization process. Multiple authorizers may include universities, uniquely created state agencies, non-profit organizations, mayors and local districts to authorize and create management structures for charter schools

Charter School Caps—State limits placed on the number of charter schools that can be authorized. Not all states have charter school caps.

Start-Up Charters—A school that is chartered as a new school, as opposed to a charter school that is converted from an existing public school.

Public School Conversions/Conversion Charter School—A traditional public school that is approved to become an independently operated public charter school. A conversion charter school is no longer under the governance of the traditional public school board, but is independently governed by its own board. State charter school legislation dictates any unique regulations that apply to conversion charter schools.

Virtual Charter Schools—A virtual school is a school in which teachers and students interact via electronic media. A virtual charter school is a virtual public school that is operated under the same guidelines as charter schools in that state.

Local Education Agency (LEA)—A legal term that defines a public school board whose responsibilities include running the school or district, taking responsibility for compliance with mandates, contracting for services and receiving grant money.

Charter School Performance Contract—A performance contract is an agreement between a charter school authorizer and a charter school that delineates the rights and responsibilities of each. This is a legally binding document that defines the terms under which the school will operate.

Charter Assistance Organizations—Organizations that assist charter schools with a variety of aspects of setup and operation. These can be offices within an existing state's Department of Education, or can be stand-alone organizations.

CHAPTER FOUR

The Face of Charter Schools

The Players and the Playing

Overview of the Chapter

In this chapter, we will look at trends in charter schools. After an overview of the role of authorizers in charter schools, we'll look at founders and see if there are trends in why they seek to open charter schools. We will also look more closely at the role that management companies play in charter school development. Then we will look closely at charter school leadership to see if there are differences between charter school leaders and traditional public school leaders in the skills that are necessary for charter school success. Our discussion will then move to teachers. What does the teaching force look like in charter schools and why do teachers opt to move away from a traditional public school to teach in charter schools? And we'll also examine why parents choose to send their children to charter schools. We will continue our discussion of the role that teacher unions play in charter schools. And finally we will look at what makes the operation of charter schools unique.

Charter School Authorizers

In chapter 3 of this primer we discussed the role of charter school authorizers in the larger picture of state legislation, accountability and advocacy. Here we will look at charter school authorizers in the more intimate relationship that they have with the schools that they charter. The relationship between a school and an authorizer begins before the school is even a school. In states where there are multiple authorizers, schools may be able to choose the authorizer to whom they apply. In single authorizer states, or states where there is no choice in authorizer, that is not the case.

Authorizers publish applications and application guidelines for founding groups who wish to apply for a charter. Authorizers or state charter school associations are typically available to answer questions and provide guidance to those applying for charters. Oftentimes, authorizers conduct interviews with potential founders as part of the authorization process.

Once a charter is granted to successful applicants, the authorizer is the main contact for accountability measures as defined by state law. It is the authorizer's job to assure that the school is compliant with the laws and policies governing charter schools. Authorizers require charter schools to report on accountability measures at least annually. Additionally, authorizers evaluate their schools' effectiveness and make decisions about charter renewal or revocation.

While this relationship can seem daunting and based strictly on compliance, the authorizer's main goal is to assure high-quality public charter school choice. So in addition to compliance and accountability requirements, the authorizer also typically provides guidance to charter schools to assure a successful program.

Charter School Founders

Let's imagine a few scenarios:

Scenario 1: Parent dissatisfaction leads to the development of a new charter school.

A parent has four school-age children. The youngest child is about to enter kindergarten. The oldest child is off to high school in the fall. The middle children are entering grades 3 and 7. The children have been enrolled in the district public school system for the past nine years. During that time, they have had some very good teachers and some not so great teachers. They have learned enough to pass from one grade to the next. Their principal seems to care. However, there have been some concerns.

The child who is entering grade 7 has struggled with understanding mathematics. The parent has spoken to the teacher on various occasions. The teacher has given the parent additional work to do with the child at home. She said that she will try to give the child extra attention during math time, but there are so many students who are struggling that she really can't spread herself that thin. She explains that she has to continue to move from one lesson to the next because she has to keep up with the district-mandated pacing guide. Without covering the appropriate number of lessons, the district has told the teachers that the students will not be able to pass the state assessment at the end of the year. With sincere apologies, the teacher tells the parent that her hands are tied because of this district mandate.

The parent approaches the principal. Actually the parent has to make an appointment to see the principal because he is often out of the building at district-level meetings. Once the parent is able to get in to see the principal, he sympathizes with the situation. He knows that the math curriculum is not meeting the needs of many children. However, the district chose this curriculum and they have paid a handsome sum of money for the materials. The district had to cut back a bit on the professional development training for teachers in the new model of instruction because the materials were so expensive. There was not enough money left for the teachers to be trained in using the materials. He is hoping that some teachers will volunteer to come in over the summer on their own time to work on strategies to better deliver instruction. He backed up the teacher's claim that the district-mandated pacing guide must be followed. He was required to report on pacing progress to the district weekly. If teachers were not where they needed to be in the instructional pacing process, there would be district-level sanctions against the teachers who were falling behind and the principal for letting it happen. He apologized and recommended that the parent take their child to one of the fee-based tutoring centers to get the extra help needed to

be successful in mathematics. He said that many other parents have done so with excellent results.

The parent goes home frustrated. How could this be happening? How could so many children in her son's class be struggling in math and nothing is being done about it? How come the child's caring teacher had to apologize for not being able to help the child? And how come the children's principal recommended that the parent go PAY someone to help tutor the child in math? Wasn't that the job of the public school system? Wasn't that what tax dollars were being spent on—quality public education?

First things first, the parent gets the child to the fee-based tutoring center. He is tested. They tell the parent that there is nothing wrong with his learning and that many children are struggling with the new curricular model being implemented in your district. The parent pays the fee and the tutoring begins.

The parent can't let this go on much longer if so many students are struggling. She goes to the next school board meeting to voice her complaint and is given three minutes to speak at the microphone. She is among 45 members of the public who are going to do so that night. She is number 38 on the list. People speak about busses failing to pick up their children, about potential school closures, about unresponsive principals, about really great principals. They speak about ideas they have for implementing various programs in the school. Now it is number 38's turn. The crowded room is hot and people have now been listening to comments for over 100 minutes. The parent speaks about her concern about the new math curriculum and the unreasonable expectations for pacing. Board members are shuffling papers, whispering questions to each other or to the staff, leaving their seats to get a bottle of water. Some of them are looking at the parent. One might be looking at her sympathetically. The buzzer goes off and the three minutes are up. The sympathetic one says thank you.

Nothing comes of this presentation to the board. The board members care about the district, but they have full-time jobs in other areas. They are not experts on curriculum. And they have other pressing issues to deal with at the board meeting. The sympathetic-looking board member asks the Superintendent to have his curriculum people look into this concern. The Superintendent states that the pacing guide was recommended by the publisher. This is a research-based mathematics curriculum, and that the only way to maintain control over learning in a district of this size was to require standardization of instruction. Nothing more is said about this concern.

Over the next year this parent shares her concerns with other parents. She finds that some teachers are also frustrated about this situation. They are professionals who want to teach children, but often feel like they are treated as robots needing to follow orders more than differentiate instruction. The parent and others start to hear about charter schools. There are some in the area. Some of the charter school parents tell stories of their schools being able to change curriculum when it isn't meeting the needs of children; of principals whose sole responsibility is the school and school program. These principals meet the children at the door, are rarely out of the building, and have an open door policy. The charter school parents are surveyed about their satisfaction every year, and results from those surveys are acted upon.

The dissatisfied public school parent and her group of similar-minded counterparts know that they are interested in another option for their children's education. They did not want to send their children to a religious-based school, nor did they want to pay the tuition associated with private education. They looked into the charter school model after hearing about local charter schools. After looking into sending their children to an existing charter school, they found that the enrollment in the charter was already at full capacity. It was obvious to them that there were not enough charter schools in the area to fill the demand by parents. They approached the state charter school association for assistance in developing an application to open their own charter school.

Scenario 2: The need for a high-quality workforce leads to the development of a charter school

A woman owns a local health care services business. The business focuses on a variety of health care service issues—home health care assistance, medical equipment rental and sales, and coordination of health services for patients. She needs a labor force that is widely varied in their skill levels. She needs college-educated employees in management positions. She needs high school graduates with clean driving records to deliver supplies. She needs health care aides with at least a high school diploma, but some college would be nice. Most importantly, these workers need to understand what it means to be a responsible worker—someone who comes to work on time and has a good work ethic.

It is difficult to find such workers. It seems that recent graduates with high school diplomas had something missing in their high school preparation. They were not ready to be productive employees in the workforce. Their attendance was sporadic. They didn't know how to communicate with their managers or peers. And they didn't have the same sense of urgency in their work as workers twenty years ago.

The discussion comes up at a meeting of local business people. They can't seem to tap into the labor force that they need. And they are not sure why.

A visit to a few local high schools for recruitment fairs helps them to see part of the problem. Discipline seems to be lacking. Many students seem to be wandering the hallways while classes are supposed to be in session. There seems to be no consequence for such behavior. There is graffiti in the hallways and restrooms. The recruiters see students talking back to teachers and the teachers backing down. One recruiter sees a student threaten a teacher. When walking past a classroom with an open door, a recruiter sees a teacher reading from overhead projector slides. The slides are yellowed with age, indicating that not much has changed in this teacher's way of teaching. Some students are sleeping. Some are reading the newspaper. Three in the back are playing cards. The teacher doesn't notice. The recruiters don't get many applicants—or even much interest—in their companies from these students. They don't really seem to be focused on what is going to happen after high school.

Not all of the schools are like this. The recruiters have recruitment fairs at some schools where teachers are teaching at the cutting edge of instruction. They are engaging the students in exciting activities that have strong connections to real-life activities. Students seem to have respectful relationships with their teachers. Teachers greet students at the door of class. The principals at these high-quality schools can be seen in hallways interacting with students and teachers. They can be seen in conference rooms meeting with groups of teachers, studying data; or meeting with students to hear their concerns. The recruiters do get applications from these students, although most are interested in internship opportunities or part-time work. Most are headed to college, or community college, and are not interested in entry-level opportunities for high school graduates.

These schools are all in the same district. They have similar rates of free and reduced lunch, a commonly accepted indicator of student socio-economic status. But why were the students so different? And why could these recruiters not get young people to work in their companies?

Some of the companies developed workforce training programs. They spent company dollars to train new employees in the role they would be working in, but also in how to be a good employee. They actually found that some of their employees—with high school diplomas—even needed remedial assistance in reading and mathematics at the very basic levels. These programs were expensive to run and did not always result in employment of the best and brightest workers.

The business owners met and decided that they needed to do something to get the types of employees they need to work in their organizations. They needed to have workers with the skills necessary to work full time in their companies. It was apparent that these workers were not currently available. Not wanting to discourage anyone from pursuing higher education degrees, they decided that they will try to get workers in well-paying positions who will benefit their company and they will provide college tuition reimbursement for those interested in pursuing degrees. But they were definitely tired of remediating entry-level workers in basic skills.

After exploring options to develop career-skill training programs for post-high school graduates, or students who have not graduated from high school but earned a general education development (GED) diploma, the business owners felt that they needed to work with these students at earlier levels of their educational career. They needed to have students develop a work ethic early on, and get basic skills of reading, writing and thinking, in addition to career development technical skills. They decided that the best way to do this was to create a charter school which was not only focused on career development, but also focused on providing life skills in an extended day, extended year internship program.

The business owners approach the state charter school association and ask for assistance in creating a charter school that serves children in grades 5–12. The school will have a career focus while providing a strong standards-based education. The students will be prepared for the world of work by developing strong work ethics and participating in internships throughout their program. Local companies will provide mentors to students. Expectations will be high. Students will all be prepared for college-level work upon graduation, if they wish to pursue it. But they will also be prepared to enter the workforce based on their experiences in the school.

Scenario 3: A potentially profitable business opportunity leads to the development of a charter school

A few entrepreneurs are having dinner. The discussion turns to education and charter schools. They start to talk about the financing of charter schools—per pupil funding, or a percentage thereof—for each child attending the school. Some quick mathematics made them realize that this could be a profitable venture. They had marketing expertise, financial expertise, management expertise. How hard could this be? They remembered that one of their friends from the local golf club was a retired public school principal. He could give them some advice. They decide to give him a call.

The entrepreneurs meet with the retired principal. He informs them that this is a great idea. Charter school parents are more involved, the kids are smarter—after all, they typically did better than some of the traditional public school kids. He advised them to create a large school, one that could house many students, in order to maximize the per pupil dollars they would get from the state. That's a lot of money to work with. The principal offered to be a consultant to the entrepreneurs. However, there was a problem. As a retired principal, he was limited by the amount of money he could earn in public education. The entrepreneurs had a solution. They would create a separate company connected to the charter school. The principal could work for the company and earn as much money as he wanted, since it wasn't state money he was being paid with.

The entrepreneurs (including the newly entrepreneurized retired principal) contacted their state charter school association and started the application process to start a charter school.

Scenario 4: Teacher dissatisfaction leads to the development of a new charter school

Four teachers are hired to teach in a large urban school district. This is their first teaching job. They meet at the employee orientation and become friends and colleagues. They all teach at different elementary schools, but stay in touch electronically as well as at district-sponsored events. They have many trials and tribulations in their first year of teaching, not unlike all first-year teachers. There are problems with classroom management, learning a new curriculum, writing lesson plans for the first time, and working with parents. They form an informal support group, and together they figure out strategies to deal with the problems they face. They have heard that some schools in other districts have mentoring groups for new teachers. There was no such program in the district where they taught, but they prided themselves on their self-mentoring capabilities.

One thing that the teachers found to be curious was the teachers' union in the district. They were required to join, and they did. Union dues were taken out of their paychecks every week. They attended union meetings. One meeting was for new teachers. They learned about their union contract and the responsibilities and rights they had under this contract. They also attended social events sponsored by the union. It was a great way to meet other teachers. And they thought that a food drive sponsored by the union to provide groceries for families in need was a wonderful idea. These were all such positive things that the union provided. But they were perplexed by the concept of "work to rule." It seems that there was a contract negotiation going on. The district negotiators were not negotiating in good faith. The union issued the work-to-rule order. This meant that teachers needed to obey the contract to the letter. They walked in at the appointed time, not a moment earlier. They left at the end of the school day—often together. These young teachers were taught that unity of the workforce would ensure that they were treated fairly. But the first-year teachers really wanted to spend more time in their classrooms. They had so much to do. And they wanted to attend professional development on their own time. They didn't feel that they needed to be paid to do so, they were happy that they didn't have to pay out of their own pocket for this professional development. It was like college tuition for free! But they were told by their union representatives that they could only attend such professional development if they were paid to do so at the contractual rate.

This resulted in confusion. The teachers knew that there were things they needed to do in order to make them the best teachers for their students, but they also knew that the union's message of solidarity was important for fair treatment. Fair treatment was important. As the union claimed, it did seem that the demands of the district were becoming unfair, and teachers were not being respected or appropriately compensated. Winning this battle would be good for teachers and in turn, good for students. So they joined their union brothers and sisters and worked to rule.

They completed their first year of teaching successfully. Each of these teachers received satisfactory and outstanding feedback on annual performance reviews. Yet at the end of the year, they each receive a layoff notice. They were bewildered. They didn't understand how they could be laid off. Students not only loved them, but actually learned in their classrooms. Their students had scored well on the district-mandated standardized tests and had excelled in their learning beyond that, as measured by various measures of growth including portfolios and project-based assessments. (These alternative measures of growth were developed by this team of first-year teachers. They hoped showing multiple measures of student growth would benefit the students, their teachers the following year, and the teachers themselves as they made the case that they were doing their job.) Parents respected these teachers. Once they overcame some of the trepidation of talking to parents about how to help their children succeed, they were accepted into the community of parents, even attending some PTO meetings. They had good relationships with their colleagues and their principals raved about their teaching. How could they lose their jobs?

It turns out that the union had negotiated a contract with the district. They had gotten a fair settlement for teachers. There were going to be salary increases, including higher stipends for professional development. There were going to be opportunities for teachers to tutor students after school and be paid for it. There was going to be more teacher representation when decisions were made at the district level. The teachers had won! But there was a price to pay for that victory. Increased costs of the new contract meant that something had to be cut. And that something was teaching positions. Necessary budget cuts forced out nearly 100 teaching positions from the district. About 25 of those positions were absorbed by not replacing teachers who were planning to retire. The other 75 positions were going to be seniority based. This meant that those hired last would be the first laid off.

This was devastating for the four first-year teachers in this scenario. They had bills to pay and really felt that their jobs were secure because they were protected by their union. It was also disappointing because they wholeheartedly believed in the union's efforts at protecting teacher jobs—they just thought that that meant all teacher jobs.

After spending a few weeks recovering from the shock of the layoff, the teachers started talking with some of their friends from graduate school who had taken jobs teaching in charter schools. These teachers were busy getting their classrooms ready for the next year. They had received offer letters from their schools, inviting them back to teach the following year. Some of them had received merit pay bonuses for meeting the school-set goals for the year. School started for them at the end of August, but that extra time was reflected in their salaries. The teachers felt that the school they taught in valued them.

The laid-off teachers tried to get jobs in charter schools after receiving their layoff notices. However, there were no openings in the schools. They had already filled open positions by April so new teachers could begin planning for the upcoming school year. But the charter school movement continued to intrigue the teachers who were laid off. They met with charter school principals, charter school founders, charter school teachers and charter school parents. They talked about what it was like to start a charter school, the resources that were available to do so. They talked about unique aspects of charter school leadership and the development of programs based on student needs. They learned that parents were interested in additional options for their children.

They also met with union leaders in charter schools. Through these discussions they learned that it was possible to have a union that represented teachers, but wasn't so big that the purpose of education got lost in the shuffle.

They had serious discussions about what they would like to offer to students in an ideal world where district-level bureaucracies wouldn't inhibit them. They decided to take a

chance and contacted their state charter school association to ask for assistance in developing an application to open their own charter school.

Not Too Much in Common

These four scenarios are very real. They represent ways in which founding boards come together and create charter schools. The scenarios are pretty diverse in rationale for starting a school. And one could imagine that in playing out any one of these scenarios further, there would be very different schools created and very different outcomes for students in those schools. The school started by the parents would probably be heavy in parental involvement and empowering teachers to meet the needs of students. The school started by local business people may have strong community partners, a professional dress code, and opportunities for internships. The curriculum would have a career focus and you can almost imagine students sitting at boardroom conference tables instead of desks. The entrepreneurs would run a school in which they were able to make a maximum profit. We can hope they turn that profit into better opportunities for children, but there wasn't too much talk about children—except as per pupil income—in their scenario. And the laid-off teachers might create a charter school with a strong union that protected teachers, and included exciting learning experiences, solid assessments of student learning, and mentoring for new teachers.

It is hard to generalize about charter school founders. They each come to the table because of a unique concern. Some have concerns about reforming a larger system. Some have concerns about better opportunities for students. Some have concerns about appropriate, cutting-edge instruction and research-based practices. And some just want to offer an option to families that is better than the options currently available in the traditional public school district. But suffice to say that in order to start a charter school, the founders group must be passionate about their purpose in doing so, because starting a charter school is no easy task.

The website for U.S. Charter Schools (www.uscharterschools.org) has created a start-up brief to indicate the steps involved in starting a charter school. They outline four steps: exploration, application, pre-operations, and operations. During the exploration phase of the charter school start-up process, it is recommended that potential founders should investigate state laws and policies. These policies may change over time, so founders must be aware of current, as well as proposed policies that effect charter schools.

Founders also need to review chartering agency policies. In states where multiple authorizers of charter schools are in place, founders should choose to apply for authorization through an authorizing agency whose philosophy most closely matches that of the founders' vision. A core founding group should be organized to plan the school and write the application. Skills of the core founding group should include curriculum, instruction and assessment; marketing; governance; finance and budgeting; education law; and some skill in writing a charter school application. Groups should also design a comprehensive school plan. This plan should include the school vision and mission; instructional program; leadership structure (governance and school administration); staffing; facilities planning and a budget.

In USCS's second phase, the founding group should be writing the actual application. In this phase, charter school founders should consult their authorizing agency of choice for specific direction on the writing of the charter application. Some states require evidence of community buy-in or district approval for a charter to be approved. Some authorizers require an interview with the founding team. There are some common elements to a quality charter school application. There must be a clear mission statement, a statement of need, a strong academic plan, a clear business model, a governance structure that assures appropriate oversight, policies for personnel, students and families; enrollment goals; potential facility; plan for insurance coverage, and a plan for monitoring, evaluating and renewing the process.

Once the charter for the school is approved, USCS recommends a plan for pre-operation of the school. Working backward from the first day of school, the founders must come up with a timeline for all issues associated with the opening of a new school. Any contracts for services must be formalized. Bylaws and Articles of Incorporation must be filed. Staff and students must be recruited. Any instructional materials must be purchased. A school facility must be procured and procedures must be put in place for accounting, budgeting, banking, payroll, etc.

The fourth phase is actual operation of the school. During this time, the school founders should be involved in the formal opening of the school, including any ceremony that might go along with such a grand event. Troubleshooting and making improvements is an inevitable part of the start-up. The governance structure needs to move from start-up to policy development and oversight. And data needs to be collected, interpreted and shared in order to make informed decisions at the instructional, structural and policy levels. (U.S. Charter Schools report, http://www.uscharterschools.org/cs/r/view/uscs_rs/1699, retrieved 6/5/2011).

This start-up outline gives a brief overview of the work involved in the creation of a charter school. And once the school is open, the real work of governance begins. The level of commitment necessary to sustain the effort of starting a charter school is great. No one person would likely possess the expertise to open a school on his or her own. Rather it takes the commitment of a group of like-minded people with a passion for the mission of the proposed charter school to get a school opened. Typically, the founding group is volunteering their time to the opening of the school. Small start-up grants are often available once a charter has been approved. But the application writing and community activism are often simply a labor of love and commitment.

The Role of Charter Management Organizations in Charter Schools

It is easy to imagine that an organization with experience in opening charter schools would be in a better position to open a charter school than one of the groups in our scenarios. In our scenarios, the charter school founders are local stakeholders driven to action by conditions that affect them. They have no experience with running a school. They have no experience with applying for a charter. But what they do have is purpose and a strong understanding of the community. This gives them a strong advantage in building a successful school model that is truly based on the needs of students. In cases like this, there may be organizations that can assist in the development of an application. Depending on the state in which the charter school will open, various levels of assistance are available for founders. States may provide resource centers that can help with application development. Most states provide technical assistance manuals to provide guidance in application development. Individual and group consultants can also provide assistance for application development; however, this assistance usually comes with some financial commitment.

Once a charter school is opened, the scope of work necessary to run a school is immense. The bureaucracy that many school founders seek to escape from is suddenly understood in a different way once a charter school begins its operation. The bureaucracy, although some would argue is somewhat cumbersome in its current iteration, was developed to meet the demands of various mandates in education. Some of the services provided by a **district central office** in a traditional public school system would be welcome in charter schools. Understanding, updating and compliance with special education regulations is something that typically happens at a centralized level in a traditional public school district. At a charter school, that work has to happen at the school level. Similarly, payroll and human resources functions that find economies of scale in a centralized system are the responsibility of individual charter schools. Additionally, purchased goods and services for a district tend to have quantity discounts applied. Charter schools are typically purchasing for a smaller population, and may not qualify for such discounts.

Seeing the need for assisting at a centralized level on behalf of public charter schools, **Charter Management Organizations (CMOs)** began to form. CMOs are organizations that work to manage public charter schools and provide some of the benefits of a district central office. CMOs are non-profit organizations. They are typically concentrated in big cities. An interim report on the effectiveness of CMOs (Lake, Dusseault, Bowen, Demeritt and Hill, *The National Study of Charter Management Organization (CMO) Effectiveness—Report on Interim Findings*, 2010) finds that CMOs use different approaches in their work with charter schools. They report that CMOs typically don't operate more than seven schools, but most have plans to operate more than they are currently operating. They tend to work from replication models of schools that have proven to be successful in other areas. The interim report finds that

---

District central office

The administrative offices in a school district responsible for tending to the business of the school district, but typically has no regular contact with students.

Charter Management Organization (CMO)

Non-profit organizations that can be contracted with to manage public charter schools and provide some of the benefits of a district central office.

CMOs tend to be prescriptive in various areas of school operation, and this prescriptiveness tends to manifest itself in assistance for struggling students, and teacher evaluation and compensation.

While CMOs may sound like small, charter school districts, Lake et al. have found that increased instructional time, teacher accountability, and performance based compensation systems to be some of the differences between CMO centralization and traditional public school district centralization. CMOs face challenges, including finding enough qualified teachers and stabilizing their workforce in light of rapid burnout.

Educational Management Organization (EMO)

For-profit organization that can be contracted with to manage public charter schools and provide some of the benefits of a district central office.

Educational Management Organizations (EMOs) are similar to CMOs; however, EMOs are for-profit organizations. EMOs provide contracted services to school districts and charter schools. A 2003 study by WestEd looked at trends and best practices of EMOs. The study found a balance of aspects of charter school choice that would support EMO growth, and other barriers to the growth of these for-profit organizations. They concluded that EMOs can add value to charter school programs. They provide services that would be difficult for charter schools to afford on their own. And they provide expertise in areas that are a challenge to many educators. The WestEd report concludes that while EMOs provide potentially beneficial services to charter schools, they do so only when used wisely by those who contract for these services (Hentschke, Oschman and Snell, *Trends and Best Practices for Education Management Organizations—Policy Perspectives*, 2003).

Assistance comes at a price for these services provided to charter schools. One reaction to this pay-for-service model, whether from a for-profit or non-profit organization, is that public school dollars meant for educating children are actually benefitting adults. In analyzing this response, one must take into account that these organizations are providing services that are currently provided in traditional public school districts. If a human resources professional in a traditional public school district collects a salary for his work, why wouldn't an external organization providing the same service deserve the same compensation? And what if the external organization provided superior services for less cost? Wouldn't that be a better use of taxpayer education dollars? A proponent of a market economy model for educational service provision might argue that introducing market competition to traditional central office bureaucracies might increase service levels for all public schools, not merely public charter schools. And increased high-quality service at lower costs would mean that more administrative dollars could be spent on teachers and children.

Another reaction to the pay-for-service model is that in looking to make a profit, charter management organizations might not provide the highest quality of service. That is a picture of for-profit education that is easy to see. However, when we think about contractual services, the development of accountable contracts for competitive prices means that to stay in the business, pay-for-service organizations must provide outstanding service, or risk loss of business.

This way of thinking about public school finance is really nothing new to public education. Traditional public school districts are required to put services out to bid. Winning bids go to the lowest bidder with a sufficient quality of product. Management organizations work in the same way.

But let's return to the original founder scenarios in this chapter, scenarios of founders who are basing their decision to open and run a charter school on community need. Oftentimes, management organizations are external to a community. Without understanding the needs, and knowing the players, in the community, charter school success is threatened. Replicable models of successful charter schools don't work if the successful charter school model is based on the needs of a community that are far different for where the replication will be developed. An ideal compromise would be local provision of cost-effective services that would meet needs of a number of charter schools in the communities in which they originate.

Charter School Leaders

In taking into account the job description of a traditional school leader, one can become overwhelmed just reading the list of responsibilities:

+ Supervise all school personnel
+ Provide support for instruction to instructional staff
+ Evaluate teachers and teacher assistants through formative and summative evaluation methods

- Coordinate professional development activities based on the needs of staff and students
- Assure that all curriculum and instruction is aligned with standards
- Assure that assessment provides opportunities for improvement of instruction and learning
- Coordinate the school program, including school budgeting
- Communicate with the central office staff about needs of the school
- Complete required compliance reports
- Motivate staff
- Develop, monitor and enforce schoolwide discipline
- Oversee facility to ensure a clean and safe working environment
- Work with families and the community to advance the mission of the school
- Assure that records are kept and secured in a manner consistent with privacy laws
- Assure appropriate supplies are in place to meet the learning needs of students

If we think of the charter school leader, all of these responsibilities are included in their job description—and a few more. Keeping in mind that a charter school is truly a non-profit organization, the responsibilities of the leader of such a school take on a more business-like perspective. The charter school leader must direct the school program as described above, but must also:

- Recruit appropriate and highly qualified staff
- Work with and advise a board of education
- Oversee the development of a budget based on school mission and state regulations
- Manage finances
- Communicate with school authorizer on issues of accountability
- Recruit students and maintain a stable student population at the school
- Assure accountability with federal and state mandates

While the lists are similar, much of the work of traditional school leaders comes with the support and assistance of a central office staff. A well-run central office will assist school leadership with hiring, recruitment, direction for mandate compliance, budgeting, supply and textbook procurement, providing services for students with special needs, etc. While some charter school founders and leaders cite the demands of a central office bureaucracy as one reason for developing their own charter school program, the work of that same central office is work that must be done. The charter school leader must be able to accomplish that level of compliance and support at the school based level. The leader must either have the level of expertise to deal with such responsibilities, or be able to hire experts who can.

Most leaders of charter schools are trained in traditional school leader preparation programs. These programs are often criticized for their lax standards, admissions policies and graduation requirements (Levine, *Educating School Leaders*, 2005). If the criticisms that are lodged against these programs indicate that school leaders are not being prepared appropriately, then one can conclude that charter school leaders—with their unique required skill set—are being even less adequately prepared in these programs.

As a result of reports of lack of quality preparation for charter school leaders, some organizations have developed charter school training programs. A 2007 study by Campbell and Grubb (Closing the Skill Gap: New Options for Charter School Leadership Development) analyzes charter school leadership programs and their impact on meeting the needs of charter school leaders. The programs studied show great differences in admissions, cost, focus, and end result (certificate or degree). However, the study finds that the similarities are what make these programs different from those that prepare traditional school leaders.

The charter school leadership development programs have similar courses and methods. They found that topics most often covered in the coursework of these programs included Leadership; Personnel; Labor Relations; Charter School Law; Charter School Financial Management; Special Education; Academic Accountability; Facilities Management; Charter Renewal Processes. Looking at this list of course topics, it is clear that the content is focused on a more specific clientele than traditional school leaders.

Most of the programs for charter school leadership development are built on more applied instructional methods. Field observations are key to many of these programs.

Learning in the field, combined with studying of scholarly work, tends to yield a more robust learning experience for students. Other instructional methodologies like project-based learning, task-based learning and class discussion are used in place of lecture in these programs to engage students in high-level thinking about charter school leadership and accountability.

The authors of the study have found areas where the charter school leadership programs have an opportunity for growth. They find that the programs are not necessarily providing training in the areas that charter school leaders are struggling with the most. Various surveys of school leaders, both charter school and traditional public school, have found that these leaders tend to struggle in areas of education of diverse students, collecting and using data, strategic planning, attracting qualified teachers, engaging parents, negotiating with the district (charter specific), financial management and fund-raising. Not many of the programs adequately address all of these topics, although some are covered more readily by programs.

The charter school leader is really a leader who must incorporate skill sets from the professional fields of traditional school principal, superintendent or central office administrator, entrepreneur, and chief executive officer. Such a skill set requires a unique preparation that can be best built from a combination of real-life experiences, formal schooling and scholarship. The charter school leader must be able to meet the expectations of their board and manage those expectations within a school environment. They must be able to lead a school community comprised of stakeholder groups that include teachers, paraprofessionals, school staff, parents, students and community members. They must supervise facility maintenance and development, oversee the finances of a multi-million dollar "corporation," recruit students, recruit and hire teachers, and maintain a stable student population, and oversee the school culture. All that and lead instruction and assessment efforts to assure that all students can learn.

Models of charter school leadership vary. Taking into account all of the responsibilities that fall on the leader of the school, some schools create administrative teams that direct certain tasks to skilled leaders. In these cases, a school may have a Director position, with a Chief Academic Officer overseeing learning and assessment; and a Chief

Business Officer overseeing finance, human resources and facilities. Other schools may contract out for services that are more efficiently available from external service providers. Leadership structure in a charter school is freed from the bureaucracy of traditional school systems. And while the leadership can seem overwhelming upon initial glance, the ability to nimbly adapt to the needs of the school in the absence of a bureaucracy is important to the successful running of the charter school model.

Teachers in Charter Schools

Why would a teacher decide to teach in a charter school? There are definitely two sides to the argument. Traditionally, charter schools do not offer tenure to their teachers. In some cases, charter school teachers are not part of their state's teacher retirement system. Add to that the longer school day and longer school year of charter schools, and teaching positions in charter schools do not seem too desirable. Remember, too, that charter schools are held to the utmost accountability standards in that schools that fail to perform are closed. Independent charter schools do not have a safety net for teachers with seniority. A closed charter school means that all employees within the school lose their jobs.

And yet, teachers are teaching in charter schools and loving it. Charter school teachers are often given the professional freedom and responsibility to serve the needs of their children without bureaucratic constraints of mandated instructional programs. Because of a lack of tenure and high accountability, only those teachers who are innovative and accountable tend to stay in the school. And parent excitement and administrative support build a school community that is appreciative of teacher ingenuity.

In their analysis of the "Charter Schools in Action" project (a project of the Hudson Institute's Educational Excellence Network, supported by the Pew Charitable Trusts), Manno, Finn, Bierlein and Vanourek studied innovations in charter schools from a variety of perspectives. In looking at policy and practice issues regarding charter school operation, and the educational impact of charter schools, they indicate that one of the many lessons that can be learned from the charter school movement is the creation of schools as true professional institutions. As such, charter schools can treat teachers as true professionals and expect professional conduct from them. This sometimes gets lost in traditional public school systems, where issues of curriculum, instruction and assessment are sometimes dictated from central bureaucratic workers who have little connection to the teachers, parents and families they are supposed to serve. In charter schools, professionalism manifests itself in the allowing of autonomy of decision making regarding instructional programming, resource allocation, staff selection, professional development, schedules, etc. In such professional environments, the end results of student learning and parent satisfaction are the indicators of success. The school leadership and staff are allowed to make professional decisions based on the end result of student learning and school accountability.

Podgursky and Ballou (*Personnel Policy in Charter Schools*, 2001) studied the personnel policies of charter schools. Personnel policies are obviously compliant with state laws governing charter schools, and therefore, as in other issues about charter schools, it is difficult to make statements about national trends. Some states, for example, allow charter schools to hire non-certified teachers. Other states do not allow this. Some states may have specific requirements about charter school teachers and collective bargaining, while states may be silent on this issue. In their survey of administrators of 132 charter schools in seven states with strong charter school laws at the time of the study, their overall findings suggest that teachers in charter schools were generally teachers who were newer to the profession and early on in their teaching careers. The ratio of students to full-time teachers was generally lower, with charter schools employing more part time teachers and teacher aides. They found high rates of teacher turnover—higher than in public schools, and more similar to the teacher turnover rates in private schools. Many teachers in the surveyed schools were dismissed for poor performance. Additionally, most of the teachers were hired and worked under one-year contract agreements, with very few charter schools having formally negotiated collective bargaining agreements. The researchers found that nearly half of the charter schools used a merit pay system to reward teachers. Overall, they found that those schools that were authorized by outside agencies (state boards or higher education institutions) were more innovative in the creation and use of personnel policies than those schools that were authorized by local school districts.

In their examination of charter school research to find trends in autonomy, accountability and performance outcomes, Bulkley and Fisler (*A Decade of Charter Schools: from Theory to Practice*, 2003) find that teachers are generally satisfied or very satisfied with their experience teaching in a charter school, but in one study found that satisfaction rates did not trump feelings that teaching in a charter school was an overwhelming experience. They posit that this dichotomy may help to explain the higher levels of teacher turnover in charter schools. Bulkley and Fisler note that teacher empowerment is a measure of satisfaction, and cite Bomotti, Ginsberg, and Cobb's 1999 study of Colorado charter school teachers, stating that teachers generally felt more empowered within their classrooms in the areas of teaching and learning, but less empowered within the school environment regarding issues of school support and facility.

In their exploratory research studying why teachers choose to work in charter schools, Malloy and Wholstetter (*Working conditions in charter schools: What's the appeal for teachers?*, 2003) surveyed 40 charter school teachers in six urban charter elementary schools. They asked the following three questions:

+ What are the working conditions for teacher in charter schools?
+ Why are teachers attracted to charter schools?
+ Are charter school teachers satisfied with their experiences?

They found that teachers are attracted to work in charter schools for education-related reasons and colleague-related reasons. Their interviews with teachers confirmed research studies finding that teachers perceive working in a charter school as an opportunity to work in an educational setting with increased freedom, flexibility and empowerment. They also wanted to work in schools with a shared educational philosophy. Teachers interviewed cited being freed from district curriculum and mandates, and given freedom to make instructional decisions based on the needs of their students. They also like being able to make decisions about their own professional development.

From the perspective of colleague-related reasons to teach in a charter school, teachers reported satisfaction with working with people who shared their vision of curriculum and instruction. Charter school teachers reported that an environment of communication and collaboration was evident in their building. Opinions were valued, and a common focus on student learning was pervasive. Many also reported that they enjoyed working with qualified and dedicated teachers who were motivated and committed to work on behalf of children.

In conclusion, the incentive for teachers to work at charter schools must be examined from a balanced perspective. The issues that keep some from the charter school experience are the opposite side of the coin for those who are drawn to teach in charter schools. A lack of a tenure system means a risk of no job security, but ensures dedicated and motivated teachers are colleagues in the school. The longer school day and school year may be burdensome, but may result in increased opportunities for student learning and inclusive decision making. High teacher turnover equals an unstable employment environment, but turnover based on dismissal of underperforming teachers means that your colleagues will be high performing and motivated. The lack of a central bureaucracy means that the burden of instructional decisions will most likely fall on the charter school teacher, but this also give the charter school teacher the ability to make instructional decisions based on the needs of students. Teachers must consider the advantages and disadvantages of working in the charter school environment in order to make a decision that will best suit their teaching philosophy.

Parents and Students of Charter Schools

One cannot refute the fact that there is a difference between charter school parents and traditional public school parents. Charter schools are public schools, but they are public schools that students must enroll in—schools of choice. Parents are typically assigned to their traditional public school based on their address. Children are required to go to that school. Transportation is provided. There is no choice or application involved.

For a parent to enroll their child in a charter school, there is some work to be done. Parents must learn about the school. They need to learn about the enrollment process.

The enrollment must be open to all students, with some preferences given for residency, sibling preference, or at-risk status. The open enrollment sometimes results in the need for a lottery of applications to determine who will attend the school. Parents must not only fill out the appropriate enrollment application by the appropriate date, but they must also be prepared to anxiously wait to see if their son or daughter gets to attend the charter school if the enrollment application number exceeds the seat count for the school. This level of commitment necessary for enrollment of one's children in a charter school takes time and energy and knowledge of the process. It is the difference in automatic enrollment by matter of law, and application enrollment by matter of choice, that does equate to some natural identification of charter school parents as being more involved in their child's education.

But this should not negate the involvement of traditional public school parents in their children's education. Children in public schools are not necessarily there because their parents don't care enough to send them to charter schools. Traditional public school parents may have made that choice based on myriad reasons: satisfaction with the traditional public school system, child's siblings or friends attend the traditional public school, proximity of traditional public school to home, quality of extra-curricular programming of traditional public school, etc. These reasons for traditional public school enrollment negate the idea that parents whose children attend charter schools care more. It is simply unsubstantiated. Parents have a variety of reasons for choosing the best school for their children.

In investigating the reasons that parents chose a charter school for their students, researchers evaluated why parents chose open-enrollment charter schools chartered by the State Board of Education in Texas. They found that no matter the racial/ethnic group or income group of the parents, the majority of parents chose charter schools to provide a better quality education for their children and provide their children with a small class size educational environment. Parents also chose these schools because they perceived them to be safer. Location was also a factor in parent choice—and more so among parents who had fewer resources to transport their children long distances to school (Kleitz, Weiher, Tedin, Matland, *Choice, Charter Schools and Household Preferences*, 2000).

There is concern that school choice models like charter schools will result in racially resegregated schools. Weiher and Tedin (*Does choice lead to racially stratified schools?*, 2002) study this issue by comparing the expressed preferences of those who chose charter schools for their children's education and looking at their behavior in actually making the choice for the children. Through interviews with over 1,000 charter school parents in Texas, the researchers found interesting results. No group of respondents said that it was important for their children to attend a school based on the racial or ethnic makeup of the school. However, there were differences between racial/ethnic groups when asked what they prefer when choosing a school. Caucasian parents cited test scores as the most important consideration in choosing a school for their child. African American parents wanted schools that taught moral values. And Hispanic parents interviewed indicated that good discipline was the most important factor in school choice. After conducting a sophisticated statistical analysis of their data, the researchers found that simple statement of preference does not have much merit. Rather, one must look at stated preference and compare it to behavior. While no one racial group indicated that race was an important indicator in school choice, behavioral patterns show race being a heavy predictor of school enrollment. In this study, African American students tended to be enrolled in schools that had a higher concentration of African Americans than the schools they attended previously. The same was true for Caucasian students and Hispanic students. And while a majority of the interviewees said that high test scores were an important factor in school choice (60.6%), the vast majority with that high test score preference actually enrolled their students in schools whose academic performance was worse than their previous school's performance. So while preference toward racial resegregation may not be a stated outcome of parental preference, school choice behavior of parents may, in fact, lead to unintended racial self-segregation in this particular study.

Parental choice is important in education. Federal legislation recognizes that parents whose children attend failing schools must have a choice to remove their children from those schools. And many parents do. Parents can choose to move children within a district, to a charter school, and if finances and preference allow, to a private school. Recruitment efforts at charter schools should address issues of access of enrollment for parents, so that the charter school parent population will mirror the parent population in the traditional public school district. Many states give guidance in this, legislating that charter school populations must mirror traditional public school populations in percentages of at-risk student populations.

What Is the Relationship between Charter Schools and Teacher Unions?

When thinking about charter schools and teacher unions, initial thoughts are often that charter schools are an anti-union movement. While this may be the case among some charter school advocates, evidence points in a different direction. In this section we will look at some evidence that some charter schools are created in response to what can be seen as anti-union sentiment. However, other charter schools embrace teacher unions and collective bargaining. And some teacher unions actually embrace the public charter school model in the creation of educational environments.

As we refer back to some of the initial discussions of the initiation of public charter schools as discussed in chapter 2 of this primer, we see that the public charter school model was initially proposed by Ray Budde and embraced by a union member, president and advocate, Albert Shanker. His frustration with school administration squashing the enthusiasm of excited and energized teachers led to his support of a union-approved school run by teachers. Charter school philosophy has its basis in pro-teacher, pro-union tenets. The idea that teachers should take control of education because they are the ones working most closely with students makes sense. It is the ultimate in fair treatment of teachers as professionals within school environments.

Certainly the idea of chartering schools has moved from the initial ideas of Shanker and Budde. Charter schools have become educational enterprises that are surrounded by controversy. Some charter schools are run by for-profit organizations, giving the impression that market competition is the basis of public education. And market competition is antithetical to the union ideal that teachers should be represented by one voice to ensure high-quality education for all students. Keep in mind, too, that state law governing charter school participation in collective bargaining agreements is what guides charter school involvement in such. According to a state charter school law analysis on collective bargaining conducted by the National Alliance for Public Charter Schools, of the forty-one states with charter school legislation, two states have laws that require charter schools to be part of existing collective bargaining units. Five states require charter schools to be part of existing collective bargaining units, but schools can apply for exemptions. In eleven states, some, but not all, schools are exempt from collective bargaining agreements. In five states some schools are exempt from collective bargaining agreements, but those that are not can apply for exemptions. And in eighteen states, charter schools are not required to be part of district collective bargaining agreements (http://charterlaws.publiccharters.org/charterlaws/component/14, retrieved July 10, 2011). No state legislation prevents schools from collective bargaining, but instead focuses on whether the collective bargaining is in line with existing district collective bargaining agreements. (The only exception to this is Texas which is an at-will state and collective bargaining is not allowed. Within their charter school legislation, Texas law indicates that district-authorized charter schools must comply with district personnel policies. State-authorized charter schools in Texas are exempt for compliance with those district level personnel policies.)

Lobbying efforts by teacher unions to block enactment of charter school laws or authorization of charter schools are legendary. As noted above, almost all states allow collective bargaining in charter schools, but the majority of state charter school laws provide exemption, or the ability to apply for exemption, from compliance with the district collective bargaining agreement. This departure of some schools from unionized collective bargaining has the potential to weaken the unions' united voice.

As we remove our discussion from the politics of teacher unions and charter school philosophy (see chapter 3 of this primer for a more detailed view of the role of politics in charter schools), we will instead look here at the role that teacher unions play in charter schools. We can look at this from various perspectives. We will look at each of the following scenarios anecdotally and assume that the school is full compliance with their state charter school legislation regarding collective bargaining. Four scenarios will be discussed—schools where teachers do not participate in collective bargaining because there is no desire for such an agreement among the staff; schools where teachers choose to create their own internal collective bargaining agreement; schools where teachers choose to collectively bargain with a state or national affiliate; and schools who are required to participate in the district's collective bargaining agreement. We will look at possible conditions that lead to the school's choice of unionization, benefits of the choice, and potential problems in each.

When we examine the research about why teachers choose to teach in charter schools, we find that they appreciate the collegiality, sharing of philosophy, open communication, and freedom and flexibility that teaching in a charter school brings. When such a program is skillfully designed, there may be no need for collective bargaining. Skillful design of such a program includes the involvement of teachers in every aspect of planning. Teachers would be involved in setting instructional program, developing calendars, choosing compensation packages like salary and benefits. Additionally, teachers would be involved in governance through an elected seat on the board of directors with full voting rights. A method for voicing concerns and complaints would be developed and teachers would have their voice heard in the school program. In this scenario, teachers share in the planning, implementation and accountability of the program. Structures are in place to ensure fairness, equality and vertical communication. This careful planning can result in an educational program that not only meets the needs of students and parents, but also takes into account the working environment for all school staff in a very proactive manner.

Problems can exist in this non-unionized scenario. There is the potential that not all teachers will be fairly represented. Favoritism could exist within the group of teachers who are participating in the creation of the working environment. Others can be left out of that planning and not have their concerns heard in the same way as those more vocal in the process. Changes in leadership and governance can also change the work environment with no formal working agreement in place.

Another scenario to consider is one in which teachers choose to collectively bargain by creating their own **school-based internal union** with no state or national affiliation. The choice to collectively bargain in this manner can be

School-Based Internal Union

A union that is formed within a school, but not affiliated with a formal local, state or national collective bargaining organization.

due to a variety of situations. Such a plan could come as the result of teachers seeing a need for collective bargaining, but feeling confident enough in their relationship with administration and the governing board to not need the protection, input and cost of affiliation with a larger state or national organization. Typically, union leaders in a local union have some experience with negotiation and law. They may hire outside legal representation on an as-needed basis. Such legal representation may also be provided to them through an agreement with their school governing board.

Teachers and other represented school staff in this scenario may develop this union as a matter of general interest to increase formal communication with the governing board. They may also create this internal union as a result of some perceived workplace infraction committed by administration or the board. Or they may create an internal union based on the requirements of state law or authorizer recommendation. While the reasons for opting for such a local, internal collective bargaining unit are varied, the idea of local control of the unit makes it unique.

Collective bargaining within the school creates a unique focus for the efforts of the union. The union can focus on issues within the school community in a strategic and unique way. They can bring the will of the membership to the attention of the administration and the board with an intimacy that will directly influence school program and teacher rights. The common focus of the concerns of the teachers and represented staff is distinctive to the population and, as such, the impact will be directly related to the issue. Many times larger unions represent districts and states and nationwide groups of teachers. Common issues are sure to exist, and as such can be addressed by the larger groups. But issues within schools that are unique to the school can be lost in the agenda of the larger group. Local unions can better represent the concerns within the common philosophy of the charter school.

Also of benefit in this scenario is the cost of representation. Union dues can be costly. Local representation still comes with a cost, but not necessarily the cost of supporting a larger organization.

Potential problems within the school-based union scenario include a lack of expertise in union issues. School-based union leaders most likely are not fully supported by union dues. Instead they are probably teachers who take on these collective bargaining duties because they are passionate about the work. They do not necessarily have the ability to commit to this work full time as many state- and nationally affiliated union representatives do. They may also not have the expertise and training of the more seasoned state and national union leaders. Legal services and other necessary services will most likely need to be contracted out. So while the local union is cost effective, the services needed to fully represent staff may not be as available as they are in larger organizations.

A third scenario to consider is a charter school whose teachers decide to unionize and join a state or national affiliate. Here the reasons for the teachers' choice to unionize can be the same as in the second scenario of locally based unionization. There may be a need to increase formal communication with the governing board. There may be perceived workplace infractions committed by administration or the board, or a general sense of mistrust or disrespect. Or they may affiliate with a state or national union based on the requirements of state law or authorizer recommendation. The difference between the reasons and implications for this more broad affiliation and a school-based union are important to note.

When teachers affiliate with a state or national union, they get the benefits of the collective expertise of the membership. This means that trained, professional negotiators are assigned for contract negotiations. Formal procedures for grievances are in place and attended by trained, professional hearing officers. The union employs its own legal staff that is experienced in labor law issues. These law professionals are available to the charter school teachers. The experience of the organization of the union is available to the charter school teachers.

There are potential problems with this arrangement. The first is that the union dues to support the larger organization of a state or national affiliate are more costly than the cost of a school-based union. These dues come as a direct cost to teachers. There is also the problem that state and national unions have an agenda that is specific to the broad body of teachers. The concerns of a national body of teachers may not be the concerns of a charter school that is exempt from many of the mandates that teacher unions fight against. In that case, the dues of the charter school teachers may be monies misspent—monies that are not directly advancing their cause. State and national unions may not yet have developed the same level of expertise in dealing with charter school issues as they have in dealing with traditional public school issues throughout their long history of representing traditional public school teachers.

And an interesting thing to note is that teacher unions have traditionally fought against charter school legislation and individual school authorizing. Yet they are taking dues from charter school teachers, even as they continue to advocate against charter school philosophy and legislation. Let's imagine that an issue is brought to the vote of an entire state union body. All members can vote. And the vote is on adopting a position on a proposed change to the funding formula for charter schools at the state level. The issue is that the traditional public school funding is jeopardized by declining enrollment due to students attending charter schools. Traditional public school teachers may feel that traditional public education needs to be funded at the same level that it always has, no matter how many families opt to send their children to charter schools. Public charter school teachers may feel that the funding should follow the child to their school of choice, and as charter school enrollment increases, money normally spent on the child's education in the traditional public school should come, in full, to the charter school. A vote of the union membership will most likely sway in the direction of the desire of traditional public school teacher perspective. Lobbying efforts and membership dollars will be spent on the will of the voting body. So charter school teachers, in this scenario, have just spent their membership dollars on an initiative that has the potential to seriously harm their school's funding. Charter schools should be cautious in their choice of state and national union representation to assure that such membership adequately represents their concerns.

And we'll now consider the final scenario of a charter school whose teachers are required to be part of the collective bargaining agreement of the district in which the school resides. In such cases, charter school founders are well aware of the constraints under which they are creating their school. They are aware that the school will need to follow the existing collective bargaining unit. And one would assume that the school founders would not take the time and effort to open a school that they felt would fail under the existing district collective bargaining agreement.

In cases like this, a charter school founding board would need to fully understand the collective bargaining contract and its implications for school culture and personnel policy. It may be that the collective bargaining agreement seems fair to the founding board and is something they can work with as they set up their school. Perhaps the rationale for the founding of the school is not to escape teacher contract issues, but rather to create a school that is unique to the choices offered within the traditional public school district. Perhaps the rationale for the founding of the school has more to do with perceived problems within the centralized bureaucracy of the district than it has to do with the teacher union contract. In this scenario, the school is founded with the compliance with the teacher union contract in mind.

Benefits of working within the existing district teacher union contract are clear. The working conditions are already set, and the school can be created with those working conditions in mind. The working conditions are created with the needs of the student population of the district in mind. The contract is not based on a faraway notion of education in the community. It is a response to the realities of the educational system in the community. The contract is also an equalizer. Most charter schools originate in communities where schools are failing and parents are looking for educational choices for their children. By following the same contract as other teachers in other schools in the district, any success of the charter school will not be "blamed" on failure to fairly represent teachers. Rather any charter school success will be realized while teachers are represented in the same way as their traditional public school counterparts, and the success can be attributed to other measures that the school employs to increase student learning.

Membership in the existing union is also of benefit when services provided by the union are needed. Legal representation and other member benefits will be available to all members, including the charter school teachers. Representation at grievance hearings and participation in union professional development activities are also of benefit to charter school teachers.

Certainly there are potential problems with working under an existing contract. If the contract is at all stringent on issues that are at the heart of the creation of the charter school (like an extended school day or extended school year), then the contract would either need to be amended for the charter school, or the school program would need to be amended to not be in violation of the contract. As with a school that affiliates with a state or national organization, the dues paid to the district may not always fairly represent the wishes of the charter school teachers if they are in the minority of the voting population. Concerns of the charter school may be unique to the charter school, or to a bloc of charter schools in the district. But if there are more traditional public schools in the district than there are public charter schools, the charter-specific concerns may be minimized by the majority population.

These examples certainly indicate that charter school teachers can be actively represented in collective bargaining agreements in a variety of ways. Care must be taken in the relationship with the union affiliate to assure that the unique needs of the charter school teachers are considered fairly as they are represented by unions.

What Is Unique about Charter School Operation?

In this chapter we looked at various people who make up charter schools. We looked at founding groups and operators and management companies, school leaders and teachers, parents and students, and teacher unions. All play a role in this educational opportunity we call a charter school. And the combination of all these unique roles results in the running of a school that is really uniquely operated. As with our examination of state laws and operators and leaders and teachers, what makes the schools unique really does vary. But a few points can be made regarding the uniqueness of this educational choice.

1. Public School Choice. By the very nature of public schools, the opportunity must be provided for all students to attend a public school. But there is rarely choice in the school that the child attends. Most public school enrollment is based on district geographical boundaries. Sometimes the size of the district limits choice. A district may only have one elementary school, one middle school and one high school. Sometimes geographical boundaries limit choice. A district may have multiple schools, but school population is limited

to children living within a certain distance from the school. In the case of charter schools, parents are given the opportunity to send their children to a specific public school that has a specific theme and philosophy. Parents are no longer relegated to the school district limitations on school program. Rather they can actively engage in choosing a public school program that meets the needs of their child.

2. Founding Groups. These schools are not mandated. In most cases, a charter school doesn't NEED to be created to fulfill state or federal mandates. (Except in some cases of persistently failing schools. Districts in which those schools exist are offered the opportunity to convert those schools to charter schools.) Charter schools are typically created by founding groups that see a need in the educational community that is not being met by the current educational system. The passion of those founding groups is what makes unique charter schools viable. They want students to learn in a different way, and they create a school to make that happen. This is not the same way that traditional public schools are created. Traditional public school creation typically rises from a growing population and the need for children in the population to receive free public education. For example, a town's population may grow due to a local industry boom. More students are admitted to the public school system. Class sizes grow. There is over crowding in the school. Another school is opened. The school meets the state and federal mandates for instruction and instructional time. This is different from the creation of a school based on a concept that is unique to an educational community and offers a different method of teaching and learning.

3. Freedom from Some Mandates. The charter school movement is built on the concept of decreased compliance with district, state and federal mandates in exchange for increase accountability for student learning, financial oversight and appropriate governance. This allows a school to be run in a way that is responsive to the unique needs of the student population in ways that larger, bureaucratic school systems cannot. Even without the mandates facing those large educational systems, there mere size sometimes prevents them from moving nimbly to meet the ever-changing

needs of students. The local governance structure of charter schools, combined with their freedom from some mandates, allows them to change instructional program quickly to meet the needs of learners. Their accountability requirements hone their focus on learning and the needs of learners.

4. Instructional Program Specifics. Charter schools are not merely schools that are complying with instructional guidelines regarding curriculum and learning activities. Instead, they are schools that can offer unique instructional programs while assuring that students meet standards. There are examples of rural agricultural charter schools where students meet standards while learning about the realities of agricultural existence. There are culinary schools where students meet the standards while preparing for careers in the culinary arts. There are technology schools where students are immersed in the world of technology as they are involved in learning programs based on required learning standards. This focus on unique instructional program is a major component in the creation of charter school models.

5. School Structure. Charter schools have the ability to structure their program in unique ways. Some have extended school days. Others are year-round schools with intermittent 10-day breaks in the program. Some are residential, providing students with on-campus living arrangements during the week. School structure is based on the mission and vision of the school and is designed in a way that best meets the learning objectives of the students in the school.

6. Based on Market Forces. Charter schools are based on market forces. They exist only when families enroll their children in the school. If parents are not happy with the educational program, they will not re-enroll their students. Without full enrollment, the school cannot meet its financial commitments and will need to restructure or close. While it may not seem right that public education is based on market forces, the concept of providing the best educational services available to meet the needs of students and families (customers) in exchange for a steady enrollment of students seems to be a fair trade-off for school operators and families.

Overall, factors leading to the creation and sustenance of charter schools are quite varied. The variance is due to state legislation, motivation for school creation, instructional program, parent choice, and school structure, among a myriad of other things. Yet the outcome is one that we all hope for in our society—the creation of good schools that meet the educational needs of our students as they prepare to become productive and caring citizens in our world. Schools created toward this end can be traditional public schools, public charter schools, private schools or home schools. Charter schools are just one method that can be employed to reach this desired end result.

Summary

In summary, there are many players in the charter school world. While each may have a unique reason for their work in charter schools, most have at their core the desire to improve education by looking at reform initiatives outside of traditional public school models. High-quality authorizers work to create compliance procedures and performance agreements that hold schools to high standards while freeing them from cumbersome and unnecessary mandates. Founders have a variety of reasons for opening charter schools. Most want to open schools that fill a need in the community. Management companies can alleviate some of the administrative burdens that charter schools face, but caution must be taken to assure the management company does not become a pseudo-central office bureaucracy that constrains charters in the same way that traditional public school district bureaucracies can constrain traditional public schools. The role of leaders in charter school is part school leader, part business person, part entrepreneur, part activist and part public relations specialist. Specialized leadership training is necessary to ensure that leaders are ready for the challenges of running this unique school model. Teachers find value in the professional learning communities of charter schools, and most are willing to give up tenure and union protection to participate in a community that has the freedom to focus on children and instruction in unique ways. Teacher unions seem to support charter schools in their policy statements, but often advocate against pro-charter legislation. Parents value a public school choice for their children, especially in communities where parents are dissatisfied with the traditional public school choice options. The unique philosophy of charter school education, in which schools are freed from compliance with certain mandates in exchange for increased accountability, is what draws people to work in or have their children attend charter schools.

GLOSSARY

District Central Office—The administrative offices in a school district responsible for tending to the business of the school district. Offices within the central office may include educational professionals who focus on curriculum, assessment, special education, English language learners, school finance, legal issues and/or public relations. Central office staff typically do not teach and are not typically in regular contact with students.

Charter Management Organization (CMO)—Non-profit organizations that can be contracted with to manage public charter schools and provide some of the benefits of a district central office.

Educational Management Organization (EMO)—For-profit organizations that can be contracted with to manage public charter schools and provide some of the benefits of a district central office.

School-Based Internal Union—A union that is formed within a school, but not affiliated with a formal local, state or national collective bargaining organization.

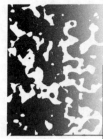

CHAPTER FIVE

Indicators of Charter School Success

Overview of the Chapter

In this concluding chapter we'll look at indicators of success of charter schools. As illustrated in chapter 1–4 of this primer, charter schools are unique in many ways. Most people see only the public persona of charter schools. They see innovations in school programs, themed schools, school uniforms, popular movies like *The Lottery* and *Waiting for Superman*. But it is the structure of charter schools, including unique governance and accountability standards, that allow them their public persona. As we look more deeply at the behind-the-scenes working of charter schools, we see that there are many indicators that contribute to their success. When the indicators are not met, charter schools may struggle and fail.

An overview of trends that lead to charter school success, as defined by the United States Department of Education and by Ball State University, a higher education charter school authorizer in Indiana, will be presented in this chapter. Then we'll conclude with an example of a successful charter school, the largest charter school in the state of New York. We'll examine the reasons it was founded; the process of opening; and its growth, challenges and successes.

Trends in Successful Charter School

When we look at successful charter schools, we could say that the implementation of a successful charter school program is no different than the implementation of a successful traditional public school program. Innovative teaching, engagement of students in the learning process, active parents, and strong leadership are all key elements of successful educational environments. But because of the two main differences in the implementation of charter school program—accountability and freedom from some mandates—a successful charter school is structured differently than a successful traditional public school. Both of these indicators are key to a charter school's success only if handled masterfully. They can also be keys to a charter school's failure if they are not addressed in a way that utilizes the freedom from mandates to achieve appropriate accountability goals.

A successful charter school community that takes its accountability goals seriously puts careful plans in place to assure that the goals are met through daily commitments to school curriculum, instruction, assessment and culture. This means that all aspects of the school program are aligned to meet the goals set forth in the charter for the school. Such schools use their freedom from various mandates to help them meet these goals. This might include implementing a longer school day or longer school year to give students extended opportunities to meet their learning goals. Other mandate exemptions might allow schools to use creative curricular and instructional approaches to meet unique needs of learners. In this way, mandate relief is directly connected to successful instructional experiences for students. Those successful instructional experiences are then directly connected to the accountability responsibilities of the school. This careful use of mandate relief, tied to accountability goals, is what makes the charter school model unique. This also requires a heightened awareness of issues associated with the governance and internal controls of the school to assure success.

In its report on successful charter schools, the U.S. Department of Education (2004) notes that there are six indicators that need to be in place for a charter school to be successful. According to this report, effective charter schools need to get a good start, lead with a mission, innovate across the school program, promote a community of continuous learning, partner with parents and the community, and govern for accountability.

By "getting a good start" the USDOE refers to the importance of a unifying vision of the school. No matter how charter schools start—whether from concerns of citizens, conversions of traditional public schools, or through experienced management companies—successful charter schools start with a clear mission and vision of the school program as dreamed by the founders.

Leading with a mission is another indicator of charter school success. A clear mission is known by all stakeholders and articulated in a variety of ways. Teachers, parents, administrators, board members, community partners and students are aware of the mission of the school. Instructional programming and school activities are aligned with the mission while goals for student success are high, yet attainable. All resources are focused on realizing the mission of the school.

Charter schools utilize their mission to focus instruction and engage in innovative programmatic design. Because charter schools are freed from certain mandates in exchange for more rigorous accountability, creativity in mission-related instructional design is possible. The school's structure and staffing can be responsive to the needs of the students and the school mission. Successful charter schools also tend to create supportive and caring environments for students. Their mission-focus results in individualized, responsive school environments in which students have many opportunities for success.

Successful charter schools also promote a community of continuous learning through internal accountability and staff commitment. Successful charters use student data—formative and summative assessments, standardized assessments, and observations—to continually monitor the instructional program. Any problems that are uncovered through analyzing the data are remediated with instructional interventions to improve student learning. Successful charter schools also tend to attract teachers who are committed to the learning of their students. The unique freedoms that are in place for instructional innovation attract

teachers who create the community of continuous learning for their students and for other teachers. This results
in an educational community that sets high standards for
achievement and works in inventive ways to help students
meet those standards.

The report finds that successful charters partner with
parents and the community. Because charter schools are a
public school choice, it is to be expected that the families
want to be a part of the school and the school community.
The schools recognize the importance of community connections and work to meet the needs of students through
addressing some concerns of families. Schools may have
family math nights, which bring families together to explore
necessary math concepts in the curriculum through games
and manipulatives. Such activities not only benefit student
learning, but create opportunities for family interaction and
school community building.

Successful charter schools also govern for accountability. Charter schools are governed by boards. The boards of
individual charter schools may have some positions that
are set aside for parents or teachers. The nature of giving parents and teachers a voice in the governing of their
school makes the decision-making authority of the boards
uniquely accountable to their stakeholders. Additionally,
the board must assure that the school is accountable to its
authorizer, and is meeting defined measures of success.
Charter schools must ensure that they are academically and
fiscally accountable in order to remain open.

Ball State University, a higher education charter school
authorizer in Indiana, has also developed a list of indicators of charter school success which expand upon those
provided by the USDOE. Schools should have a clear and
well-articulated mission that is communicated to all stakeholders, is aligned with the needs of the target student
population, and is consistent with state charter school legislation. A solid governance structure is also noted as an
indicator of success. The board of the school should consist
of members who are well qualified, with clear lines delineat-
ing their authority in school decision-making.

The importance of parental/guardian participation is
noted in the Ball State document. The participation of note
is the involvement of parents/guardians in the attainment of
the school mission as well as involvement through keeping
them informed of their children's progress.

The document also notes sound administrative management as a key to charter school success. This would include administrators who are highly qualified or certified, and experienced. Roles should be clearly defined. The number of administrators in the school should be sufficient to support the operations of the school. Policies and procedures for personnel should be clear and appropriate. And an effort should be made to retain qualified, effective staff.

If a charter school is working with an Educational Management Organization (EMO), it is recommended that a contract is in place that carefully defines appropriate roles for all parties. The school should have considered other options before selecting this particular EMO and have specified reasons for their choice of EMO. Fees paid to the EMO should be appropriate for the services provided, and the charter school board must evaluate the EMO to assure that the performance is satisfactory.

A strong educational program would have a curriculum that is aligned with the school mission and the state standards and graduation requirements. The program should be understood by all stakeholders in the instructional community, including parents. The educational program should be adapted to serve students with special needs, and have the capability to improve student learning and increase student performance on identified assessments. Additionally, it is recommended that the program have a reasonable student-teacher ratio.

Qualified and dedicated teachers are an essential part of a successful charter school. It is recommended that teachers are certified and meet the requirements of highly qualified teachers per the No Child Left Behind Act. Additionally, they should be knowledgeable and caring, and follow the school's mission, curriculum and instructional approach.

Successful charter schools should serve students with special needs. Staff should be aware of all legislation that governs the provision of services to students with special needs. Teachers and administrators should be qualified and appropriately certified to provide services to students with special needs. Students should be identified appropriately and qualified staff must be available to serve on Individualized Education Program (IEP) teams. All services provided should be consistent with legal requirements for provision of special education services.

The health and safety of students and staff in the school must be a priority. Qualified staff should be available to provide for the health of students and staff. Staff should be knowledgeable about student medical needs and provision of treatment. Medications should be handled appropriately, and first aid and emergency services must be readily available. The school should also consider the nutritional needs of students enrolled in the school as part of their plan for health and safety.

Successful charter schools show evidence of increasing student achievement. Such schools set clear annual expectations for student performance on indicated measures. Such measures may include required state assessments as well as other assessments stated in the charter. Evidence of annual increases in student performance should be given. The school should ensure that student performance meets the requirement for Adequate Yearly Progress (AYP) per the No Child Left Behind Act. Additionally, school staff should use assessment results to inform instruction and increase student learning and achievement.

The Ball State report recommends that, in a successful charter school, the school climate be conducive to learning and that clear and appropriate expectations for student behavior are in place. The expectations for student behavior should be communicated to students and parents, and consequences for inappropriate behavior are appropriate and fairly administered.

Sound financial management practices are key to a successful charter school. The financial management team must be competent and demonstrate an understanding of the state funding formula and available federal grants. Sources of revenue should be identifiable and sufficient for school operations. Expenditures should be reasonable and appropriately monitored. The school should maintain a balanced budget and the student-staff ratio should be consistent with budget costs.

Recruitment and admissions policies in charters should include that the school is open to all, that recruiting activities are fair, and that a lottery system is utilized when necessary.

The charter school should follow applicable desegregation procedures for a school of choice. A successful charter school should be viewed by parents and students as a desirable educational setting, and sufficient numbers of students should seek enrollment in the school in order for the school to be financially sound. Successful charter schools should maintain the majority of their student enrollment throughout the year, with many students returning the following year. The educational mission and instructional program should be understood and supported by all community stakeholders.

Facilities in successful charter schools should fit the educational program and be adequate for the enrollment of the school. Federal, state and local codes should be met. The facility should provide a physical space that is conducive to learning.

It is recommended that charter schools consider the transportation needs of their students and budget reasonable and appropriate costs for student transportation.

And finally, it is recommended that the charter school have a good reporting relationship with its authorizer. The school should meet all reporting requirements as outlined in state charter school law and by the sponsoring authorizer of the school.

These guidelines for successful charter schools are certainly just that—guidelines. There is more that equates with the success of charters, but by adhering to these overarching principles, school founders are off to a good start.

An Example of a Successful Charter School

Overview of the School—Just the Facts

The Charter School for Applied Technologies (CSAT) is a K-12 charter school that educates 1,650 students. It is located in Tonawanda, NY and the school stands 27 feet from the Buffalo, NY city line. There are many charter schools in the Buffalo, NY area. Buffalo has the largest concentration of charter schools in New York State outside of New York City. Charter schools tend to open in areas where parents are looking for viable public school choices for their children. Typically that means that they open in areas where the traditional public schools are failing. This is true in Buffalo, where the high school graduation rate consistently hovers around 50% and the graduation rate for black males falls near the 25% mark. (This information is as of June 2011.) Charter schools in this area provide parents and students with unique public school choice educational opportunities.

The Charter School for Applied Technologies (CSAT) is New York State's largest charter school. Most of the students at CSAT are from the Buffalo Public School System (84%). The poverty rate at the school is 82%, based on the percentage of students who qualify for federally-funded free and reduced lunches. Per NYS Charter School law, the school cannot admit students based on academic performance criteria. Instead, students are randomly selected through a lottery process that is open to all students. NYS Charter School legislation does allow charter schools to give enrollment preferences to siblings of current students and to students living within the township or city in which the school is located.

The mission of CSAT is based on a school-to-career focus. The school's motto is "Every Day Is Career Day." CSAT's school-to-career component prepares all students, including those who may not be college bound, for the world of work. Career preparation starts for students in kindergarten with field trips and visits by community business leaders and extends throughout their entire educational career, culminating in student enterprise programs, job shadowing, and individualized work study and internships for those in high school.

In spite of its non-selective enrollment processes and high poverty rate, CSAT continually posts performance results noting great success. Students in the school continually outperform Buffalo Public School students on standardized test scores. The school's high school graduation rate of 100% far exceeds the Buffalo Public Schools.

The school opened as a K–6 building in 2001. After adding one grade per year, it reached maximum capacity, educating students in grades K-12 by 2007. In 2011 the school graduated its fourth class of twelfth graders. Class size in the elementary school is 27 students per class. In grades 9–12 the average class size is 23 students per class. The school has a longer school day (7.5 hours as compared to 5 or 5.5 hours as required by New York State law) and a longer school year (191 days as compared to 180 days required by New York State law).

The school employs 110 teachers and 8 administrators. The current administrative structure consists of a Superintendent, an Assistant Superintendent, a K-12 Dean of Students, a K-8 Principal, two K-8 Assistant Principals, a High School Principal and a High School Assistant Principal.

Comparison of High School Graduation Rates in the Buffalo Public School System and the Charter School for Applied Technologies.

	Graduation Rate 2008	Graduation Rate 2009	Graduation Rate 2010	Graduation Rate 2011 (unofficial as of this writing)
Charter School for Applied Technologies	94%	100%	100%	100%
Buffalo Public School System	45%	53%	47%	No data currently available

The school has no tenure policy in place. Teachers are given one-year contracts for their first 3 years of employment. After that they get a renewable contract that spans three years. In their seventh year of employment teachers are given an Open-Ended Engagement. During this agreement, the teacher is guaranteed employment as long as the school is open, the teacher meets rubric performance goals, the teacher is not disciplined for gross misconduct, the school is financially viable, and the school does not substantially change its programs.

The charter school movement is often labeled as an anti-union movement; however, that is not the case at CSAT. Because the school opened its doors with more than 250 students in 2001, and, in accordance with state Charter School law, instructional staff was eligible, and chose, to unionize from the inception of the school. (NYS Charter Schools Act of 1998 (Amended 2010) states that non-conversion charter schools and their employees are not subject to existing district collective bargaining agreements. However, if the school opens with more than 250 students or exceeds 250 during the first two years operation are eligible to be represented in a separate negotiating unit.) Members of the school instructional staff belong to the New York State United Teachers union (NYSUT) and the National Educators Association (NEA). Instructional staff is represented by four in-house union representatives. Regular union meetings of the membership are held. Members of the union leadership describe themselves as having a nice working relationship with those in management that is marked by mutual respect and common goals of student success. Of course, there are issues that emerge as important to the union membership, such as working conditions, teacher evaluation systems, school norms and policy issues that are addressed each year.

So what makes it so successful?

Above are listed the facts that pertain to the charter school. On paper, the school looks good. It has comparable demographics to the district from which it draws, but superior results. Students continue to enroll, and a lengthy waiting list is created annually. Teachers are appropriately represented, but are still held accountable. However, the true essence of what makes CSAT successful is the culture of the school and the structures that are in place to support that culture.

Governance: CSAT is governed by a Board of Trustees. This Board is responsible for the creation of the school, hiring and evaluating the school leader, developing policy, assuring compliance with state charter school regulations and maintaining the fiscal stability of the school. CSAT Board consists of business people who are active in the community. They created this school by seeing the need for a school-to-work educational choice for parents. They wanted to create a private school-like education for students in a public school environment. The board members bring a wide range of talents to the governance of the school. Legal, financial, business and community engagement expertise are found on the board of CSAT.

When CSAT opened, the Board of Trustees had a contract with a management company. Not only did the management company set the academic program and put business office protocols in place, they also were able to fund the facilities for the school. (Facility funding is often a problem for charter schools in that they don't have enough money at their inception to fund a building. With the typical length of a charter being five years, borrowing is limited.) As the Board worked with the management company, they realized that there were some things that were of concern. While the academic program was strong, the management company was not running the business office side of the charter school as efficiently as the Board would have liked. They report that in an attempt to replace the central office bureaucracy of a large school district, the management company itself was becoming quite bureaucratic. Eventually the school separated from the management company. Because of their successful financial management practices, the Board was able to bond enough money to repay the initial facility funding to the management company.

The Board of Trustees prides itself on innovative practices in education. They oversee a high-quality academic program led by their Superintendent. They support the development and marketing of an in-house assessment data system that is now being used by public, charter and private schools throughout the United States. The Board has developed a culinary program in the high school, and has also built a commissary so they can offer high-quality breakfast and lunch programs to other charter schools. They are pursuing funding to replicate their successful charter school model. This innovative Board has created, managed and supported an outstanding school program through their expertise, passion, and vision.

Mission: The mission of CSAT is evident throughout the K–12 program. Students are dressed professionally, in the uniform of yellow CSAT polo shirts and blue pants or skirts. (The shirts, by the way, are given to students at the beginning of the year at no cost. Each student receives two shirts. Additional shirts can be purchased for a nominal price.) Halls are orderly. On any given day, students can be seen boarding busses to take trips that will give them insight into various career choices. Kindergarteners might go to the zoo—with a highlight of the trip being a meeting with the zookeeper to find out what her job entails. Middle school students might visit a nearby manufacturing plant to see the work of the organization. Or they might be seen at a local college campus exploring what campus life has to offer. In the high school, students are not only working closely with the guidance department on college applications, but also investigating various internship opportunities that are available to them.

One would not be surprised to see the school filled with adults from the community on various days. Adults from an engineering company that partners with the school may be in school that day working on paper glider designs in order for students to learn the concept of aerodynamics. A fitness instructor may be leading students in a quick Latin dance exercise routine, and then talking about her role in keeping the community fit at the local gym. Students at CSAT are surrounded by adults who focus student attention on post-secondary opportunities.

The mission of the school is communicated to all stakeholders—community members, students, families, and all school employees. Decisions are made based on adherence to the mission. It is quite obvious that every day IS career day at CSAT.

School Climate: The climate at CSAT is one that is focused on learning. All staff is professional and welcoming. The common behavior system that is in place at the school assures that all students understand behavioral expectations and consequences. Because the behavior system is universal, all staff, including office staff, nurses, cafeteria workers and facilities staff, understand the system and can reward or remind students when appropriate. This common language of behavior is a cohesive aspect of the school that unites all in the learning community.

There are many celebrations of student success at the school. All students in grades K–12 are rewarded for their success in the classroom. The rewards can be for academic growth, appropriate behavior, creativity, or ingenuity. They can take the form of a warm word of congratulations from an adult, to a picture on the reward wall, to a formal celebration of success.

This is not to say that all aspects of student behavior and learning are positive. There are problem behaviors, as there are in any school. In order to minimize disruption to the learning process, students who reach a certain level of problem behavior are removed from class and sent to the problem-solving room. The problem-solving room is staffed by professional educators and social workers who help the child to figure out the issue that caused them to be removed from class, and to work on behaviors to remedy that issue.

For students who have problems beyond what is available in the problem-solving room, a staff of counselors and social workers are available to assist students. The school operates a Family Support Center that assists families who need extra support as they help their student learn. Grants from local foundations ensure that the services at the Center are free of charge.

This climate of student focus and learning celebrates the successes of students and assists them as they pursue the educational opportunities the school has offered them.

Common Focus on Continuous Learning: The staff at CSAT has a very sophisticated understanding of the importance of using formative assessment results to inform their instruction. They operate in a professional learning community model. Teachers meet in grade-level teams at the elementary school, and in subject area teams at the high school, to discuss data from common formative assessments and make changes to instructional programs. Teachers have two common planning periods with their team daily. It is the expectation of the school leaders that teachers use one of those common planning times to focus on common formative assessment data.

The data meetings are carefully planned. Common formative assessment data is readily provided through the use of an in-house developed data analysis tool that is called eDoctrina. Teachers create common assessments, scan student work through the copy machine into the eDoctrina program, and various reports including item analysis reports are created. Through using this program, a teaching team can give an assessment in the morning, have the assessment scanned immediately after the administration of the test, have results by the afternoon, and make instructional changes where necessary before the day is over. That real-time analysis of data and discussion of instructional techniques has an impact on student learning.

An important aspect of the data-based culture at CSAT is the idea that data must be shared in order to make changes that benefit all students. This is sometimes a difficult thing for teachers to do when they are used to closing their door and "doing their own thing." However, teachers quickly learn that through their analysis of data and sharing of instructional techniques, all students benefit. An administrator of the school often shares a story of a data meeting that took place early in the school's history. Teachers seemed hesitant to share certain aspects of their data reports, especially those topics where their students did not do well. However with some administrative encouragement, the teachers did share the data. It turned out that one class of students did quite well on a certain skill, while most of the other students did not. When asked, the teacher whose students did well had used a certain manipulative that she had learned about in college to teach the skill. She shared that manipulative with the other teachers, and by the next day, all students in the grade level had an understanding of the concept. The data meeting schedule, as well as the culture of data analysis for instructional improvement, led to increased student learning.

At the high school level, students know that the school day extends until 4:00 p.m. The last hour of instruction is an intervention period. Throughout the day, teachers make note of students who may need extra help or enrichment experiences. Student names are entered into a computer. At 3:00 p.m. the students check a computer screen and see where they are to report. Some students who are struggling in math, for example, will be assigned to the math lab. Students who may have not completed a homework assignment in history are assigned to meet with the history teacher. This personalized hour of the day ensures that students are receiving the directed help that they need in order to succeed in the school's academic program.

Data are also collected at the school for programmatic assessment. When a group of teachers realized that students were struggling in math, they gathered the data and formulated a plan to create a math lab to address the needs of students. The teachers presented the data to the school's board of trustees who provided funding in support of the math lab. The decision was based on academic data to help improve student learning.

Qualified and Dedicated Teachers: CSAT is committed to ensuring that the teaching staff is highly qualified and dedicated to the mission of the school. As described above, the teachers at CSAT are not granted tenure. Instead, they receive one-year renewable contracts for their first three years of employment. After that they receive a three-year contract, and then an Open-Ended Agreement. In addition to that employment structure, teachers are also part of a performance-based compensation system at the school. The thing that is unique about the performance-based compensation system at CSAT is the focus on team performance. Each team of teachers receives the same bonus based on a specified rubric shared at the beginning of each year.

The board of trustees of CSAT worked with administrators and union representatives to develop a system to be aligned with school goals and research-based best practices. The design of the system focuses on the following key points:

1. Teachers had to feel they could impact the results, so the selected assessments had to be relevant to what they taught. They had to feel control over the end result.
2. The system had to encourage teachers to work collaboratively and support each other toward attaining the goals established and provide less emphasis on individual teacher accomplishments.
3. The system had to allow for all staff members to attain the highest performance increase. The budget is written assuming that all teachers may earn the maximum 7% raise. Thus, they are not competing against each other for scant resources for raises.
4. The system had to support the school mission which focused on school to career preparedness.

Through this system, each year staff members can earn from 4%–7% pay increases based on a four-point rubric. This system is attractive to the teachers' union because teachers at other schools typically receive 4% increases. This rubric system ensures that all staff are guaranteed at least a 4% raise. There is no potential cost to teachers for buying into the system, but there are potentially great benefits to teachers. The rubric was initially created by a collaborative stakeholder team, consisting of grade-level representatives, union representatives and administrative representatives. Rubric refinement takes place annually.

The rubric was comprised of three components: Student Achievement (60%), School Vision (20%), and Individual Efficacy (20%). The student achievement percentage of the performance-based rubric is based on agreed-upon student achievement targets for teaching teams. Typically such targets are aligned with the achievement goals stated in the charter. Standardized tests are commonly used in this category, as are school assessments, performance assessments, or other measures that the school community agrees upon. The school vision component is focused on the role of the team in contributing to the career-focus mission of the school. Teams are responsible for arranging career experiences for their students. Experiences could include in-class presenters, field trips, or internships. Level of expectation is defined within the rubric. The individual efficacy component is based on individual teacher performance reviews. Summative evaluations of teachers are rated on a 1–4 scale.

This is the only indicator in the rubric that is individually based.

The Charter School for Applied Technologies has the winning combination of smart governance, strong leadership, teacher incentives, learning climate and student support in place to lead to a successful school model. Serving a similar population to the local school district, the school continues to outperform the local school district on all indicators. While traditional schools can certainly replicate this model, the freedom from certain mandates and the strong focus on accountability inherent in the charter school model is what allows the school to work in this capacity.

Conclusion

The Charter School for Applied Technologies is one of hundreds of models of successful charter schools. As clearly stated in this chapter, the United States Department of Education and Ball State University outline similar indicators of charter school success. Clear and communicated mission; strong governance; outstanding fiscal management; qualified and innovative leadership; dedicated teachers; robust instructional program aligned with standards; community and parent involvement; and focus on accountability can all lead to success. The Charter School for Applied Technologies has addressed these success indicators throughout their program, and as such have created a school that not only meets standardized testing benchmarks, but also graduates students who are ready for the challenges of college and careers.

We can no longer say that the charter school movement is a public school experiment. Charter schools are viable alternatives to traditional public schools. Strong legislation and rigorous authorization and compliance procedures will make charter schools stronger.

As a choice within the public school arena, charter schools and traditional public schools may actually find that they can learn from each other and create public school systems that are even more responsive to the needs of students.

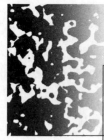

Further Readings

Articles and Briefs

Bailey, M., & Cooper, B.S. (2009). The introduction of religious charter schools: A cultural movement in the private school sector. *Journal of Research on Christian Education, 18*(3), 272–289.

Buckley, J., & Schneider, M. (2006). Are charter school parents more satisfied with schools? Evidence from Washington, DC. *Peabody Journal of Education, 81* (1), 57–78.

Buckley, K., & Hicks, J. (2003). *Educational management organizations and the development of professional community in charter schools* (Occasional Paper No. 69). New York: National Center for the Study of Privatization in Education.

Bulkley, K. (1999). Charter school authorizers: A new governance mechanism? *Educational Policy, 13*(5), 674–697.

Cannata, M. (2011). Charter schools and the teacher job search. *Journal of School Choice, 5*(1), 111–133.

Eckes, S. E., Fox, R. A., & Buchanan, N. K. (2011). Legal and policy issues regarding niche charter schools: Race, religion, culture, and the law. *Journal of School Choice, 5*(1), 85–110.

Hassel, B. C. (2005). *Charter school achievement: What we know.* Washington, DC: Charter School Leadership Council.

Hassel, B. C., & Batdorff, M. (2004). *High-stakes: Findings from a national study of life-or-death decisions by charter school authorizers.* Chapel Hill, NC: Public Impact.

Hassel, B. C., & Vergari, S. (1999). Charter-granting agencies: The challenges of oversight in a deregulated system. *Education and Urban Society, 31*(4), 406–428.

Henig, J. R., Holyoke, T., Brown, H., & Lacireno-Paquet, N. (2005, August). The influence of founder type of charter school structures and operations. *American Journal of Education, 111*(4), 487–522.

Hill, P. T., & Lake, R. J. (2010). The charter school catch-22. *Journal of School Choice, 4*(2), 232–235.

Lake, R. J., & Hill, P. T. (Eds.). (2005). *Hopes, fears, and reality: A balanced look at American charter schools in 2005.* Seattle, WA: Center on Reinventing Public Education.

National Association of Charter School Authorizers. (2005). *Principles and standards for quality charter school authorizing* (Rev. ed.). Alexandria, VA: Author.

National Center for Education Statistics. (2004). *The nation's report card: America's charter schools: Results from the NAEP 2003 pilot study* (NCES 2005-456). Washington, DC: Author.

Palmer, P. B., & Gau, R. (2003). *Charter school authorizing: Are states making the grade?* Washington, DC: Thomas B. Fordham Institute.

Renzulli, L. A., Macpherson Parrott, H., & Beattie, I. R. (2011). Racial mismatch and school type: Teacher satisfaction and retention in charter and traditional public schools. *Sociology of Education, 84*(1), 23–48.

Resnick, M.A. (2010). Department slows the race to the charter. *American School Board Journal, 197*(1), 8–9.

Smith, N., & Herdman, P. (2004). *Built for quality: The capacity needed to oversee charter schools* (Issue Brief No. 9). Alexandria, VA: National Association of Charter School Authorizers.

Thomas B. Fordham Institute. (2005). *Charter school funding: Inequity's next frontier.* Washington, DC: Author.

U.S. Department of Education. (2004). *Innovations in education: Successful charter schools.* Washington, DC: Office of Innovation and Improvement.

U.S. Department of Education. (2004). *Evaluation of the public charter schools program: Final report.* Washington, D.C.: Office of the Under Secretary.

Vanourek, G. (2005). *State of the charter movement: Trends, issues, and indicators.* Washington, DC: Charter School Leadership Council.

Wells, A. S. (n.d.). *Beyond the rhetoric of charter school reform: A study of ten California school districts.* Los Angeles: UCLA Charter School Study.

Wohlstetter, P., Malloy, C. L., Smith, J., & Hentschke, G. (2004). Incentives for charter schools: Building school capacity through cross-sectoral alliances. *Educational Administration Quarterly, 40*(3), 321–365.

Ziebarth, T. M. (2004). *Closing low-performing schools and reopening them as charter schools: The role of the state.* Denver, CO: Education Commission of the States.

Books

Berends, M., Springer, M.G., & Walberg, H.J. (Eds.). (2008). *Charter School Outcomes.* University of Michigan, MI: Lawrence Erlbaum Associates.

Brouillette, L. (2002). *Charter Schools—Lessons in School Reform*. Mahwah, NJ: Lawrence Erlbaum Associates.

Buckley, J., & Schneider, M. (2009). *Charter Schools: Hope or Hype?* Princeton, NJ: Princeton University Press.

Carnoy, M., Jacobsen, R., Mishel, L.R., & Rothstein, R. (2005). *The Charter School Dust-Up: Examining the Evidence on Enrollment and Achievement*. Washington, DC: Economic Policy Institute.

Finn, C.E, Jr., Manno, B.V., & Vanourek, G. (2000). *Charter Schools in Action: Renewing Public Education*. Princeton, NJ: Princeton University Press.

Fuller, B. (Ed.). (2000). *Inside Charter Schools: The Paradox of Radical Decentralization*. Cambridge, MA: The President and Fellows of Harvard College.

Hassel, B.C. (1999). *The Charter School Challenge: Avoiding the Pitfalls, Fulfilling the Promise*. Washington, DC: The Brookings Institution.

Hill, P.T., Lake, R.J., & Celio, M.B. (Eds.). (2002). *Charter Schools and Accountability in Public Education*. Washington, DC: The Brookings Institution.

Maranto, R., Milliman, S., Hess, F., & Gresham, A. (Eds.). (2001). *School Choice in the Real World: Lessons from Arizona Charter Schools*. Boulder, CO: Westview Press.

Merseth, K.K.., Cooper, K. Roberts, J., and Tieken, M. (2009). *Inside Urban Charter Schools: Promising Practices and Strategies in Five High-Performing Schools*. Cambridge, MA: Harvard Education Press.

Nathan, J. (1998). *Charter Schools: Creating Hope and Opportunity for American Education*. San Francisco, CA: Jossey-Bass Publishers.

Ravitch, D., & Viteritti, J.P. (Eds.). (1997). *New Schools for a New Century: The Redesign of Urban Education*. New HAve, CT: Yale University Press.

Rofes, E. & Stulberg, L.M. (Eds.). (2004). *The Emancipatory Promise of Charter Schools: Toward a Progressive Politics of School Choice*. Albany: State University of New York Press.

Sarason, S.B. (1998). *Charter Schools: Another Flawed Educational Reform?* New York: Teachers College Press.

Smith, Stacy. (2001). *The Democratic Potential of Charter Schools*. New York: Peter Lang.

Zimmer, R., et al. (2003). *Charter School Operations and Performance: Evidence from California*. Santa Monica, CA: RAND Education.

Web Sites about Charter Schools

Center for Education Reform
http://www.edreform.com/Home/

Center on Reinventing Public Education
http://www.crpe.org/cs/crpe/print/csr_docs/home.htm

Education Commission of the States
http://www.ecs.org/ecsmain.asp?page=/html/IssueCollapse.asp

National Alliance for Public Charter Schools
http://www.publiccharters.org/

U. S. Charter Schools
http://www.uscharterschools.org

Index